TA

2000

With love to Bill, Jean, Rob and Shani

This is the third year that I've written these books and it's about time I thanked all the people who help me to put them together. I have worked with some of them since the beginning of the books, and others have only recently started lending me their help, but I am immensely grateful to them all. So thank you, Nova Jayne Heath, Nicola Chalton, Nick Robinson and everyone else at Robinson Publishing for being such a great team to work with. Thanks to Chelsey Fox for all her agenting skills. And a huge thank you to Annie Lionnet and Jamie Macphail for their tireless work.

TAURUS
2000

Jane Struthers

First published in 1999 by Parragon

Parragon
Queen Street House
4 Queen Street
Bath BA1 1HE
UK

Produced by Magpie Books, an imprint of
Robinson Publishing Ltd, London

ISBN 0 75252 891 2

A copy of the British Library Cataloguing-in-Publication Data
is available from the British Library

Printed and bound in the EC

CONTENTS

Dates for 2000

Taurus 19 April – 19 May

Gemini 20 May – 20 June

Cancer 21 June – 21 July

Leo 22 July – 21 August

Virgo 22 August – 21 September

Libra 22 September – 22 October

Scorpio 23 October – 21 November

Sagittarius 22 November – 20 December

Capricorn 21 December – 19 January

Aquarius 20 January – 18 February

Pisces 19 February – 19 March

Aries 20 March – 18 April

YOUR TAURUS SUN SIGN

This chapter is all about your Sun sign. I'm going to describe your general personality, as well as the way you react in relationships, how you handle money, what your health is like and which careers suit you. But before I do all that, I want to explain what a Sun sign is. It's the sign that the Sun occupied at the time of your birth. Every year, the Sun moves through the sky, spending an average of 30 days in each of the signs. You're a Taurean, which means that you were born when the Sun was moving through the sign of Taurus. It's the same as saying that Taurus is your star sign, but astrologers prefer to use the term 'Sun sign' because it's more accurate.

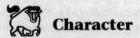 **Character**

You belong to the sign that is the salt of the earth – there's something very dependable about you. It shouldn't come as a surprise, therefore, to know that you belong to the Earth element of the zodiac, making you responsible, steady and trustworthy. It also makes you immensely practical and pragmatic, so it's no wonder that people rely on you to such an extent. You're someone who can be counted on.

Taurus is one of the Fixed signs of the zodiac, which means that you're very resistant to the idea of change. It makes you feel nervous and as if you're standing on shifting sands, and you always find it takes a long time to get used to any major alterations in your life. As a result, you tend to slip into routines that quickly become ruts, because you'd rather know what each day is going to bring (even if you get bogged down in the process) than risk unsettling yourself with disturbances to your regular schedule.

Knowing where your next meal is coming from is very important to you. You need to have your sense of self-worth and progress through life reflected in your possessions. As a result, you tend to accumulate a lot of belongings because, subconsciously, you see them as status symbols. This means you can become hemmed in by your possessions because they start to rule your life – you can't run the risk of losing all these objects that mean so much to you. As a result, you can't break out in new directions even if you want to because you're scared of what you might lose in the process. Eventually, this can feel like a straitjacket.

Some astrology books describe Taureans as slow, but it would be fairer to say that you take life at a measured pace. You do things in your own time and in your own way – and you'll simply turn a deaf ear to anyone who tries to persuade you differently. You have a magnificent sense of determination but sometimes this turns into a stubborn streak, with you absolutely set on standing your ground come what may. Nothing will change your mind and people can go blue in the face trying to talk you round but you simply won't listen.

Patience is your middle name and it takes an enormous amount of provocation to make you lose your temper. Once you do get sufficiently annoyed, however, you certainly let everyone know – and how! It's a case of light the blue touchpaper and stand well back. You can smoulder for a long time after the initial row has blown over and everyone else has forgotten all about it.

Relationships

One of your most endearing traits is your loyalty. You're a devoted friend and you probably have a select circle of very close chums that you've known for a long time rather than a wide range of acquaintances. It takes you a while to get to know people properly and they have to earn your trust, but once they've done that you become a steadfast and staunch pal who will stand by them through thick and thin. They know they can count on you in a crisis.

Your family are very important to you and you devote a lot of time to them. You feel comfortable around these people because you've known them for such a long time and you probably enjoy keeping up long-standing family traditions, especially at festive times of the year.

Taureans are very loving and affectionate, but there's a darker side to the picture. Unfortunately that delicious depth of affection can sometimes turn into something extremely unattractive – a tendency to be possessive. You can act this way towards friends and family as well as your partner, making it plain that you consider them to be your property. You may hate to let them out of your sight or you may object when other people lay claims on their time. Sadly, this is usually self-defeating because the person concerned won't enjoy being treated as if you own them, and as if they're out on loan whenever they're away from you. If this possessiveness gets very pronounced, the person may run fast in the opposite direction. Sadly, this may make you even more determined to cling on to the next person that you fall in love with. If you could only learn to let go, and understand that the best way to keep someone's love is to give them their freedom, you would be a lot happier.

Money

You have a natural affinity with money, and it plays an important role in your life. You find it reassuring to know there's enough money in the bank for a rainy day. Your practical nature stands you in excellent stead when it comes to money matters, because you always do your best to keep your finances up-to-date and in good order. Savings schemes appeal to you, and you probably began to deposit regular amounts of money into your piggy bank from an early age. One of the first things you like to do when you've got the money is buy a home of your own. It makes you feel safe to know that you've got a roof over your head and that you aren't giving your hard-earned cash to a landlord. Instead, you've got an investment for the future, and you're also creating a comfortable home at the same time.

It's important for you to make adequate financial provision for the future, such as investing in a solid pension and salting away any spare cash into reliable savings accounts. But this doesn't mean you're miserly or tight-fisted – on the contrary, you can be the soul of generosity and enjoy sharing what you've got with your loved ones. You also like treating yourself to luxuries and treats, especially if they're intended to pamper you or help you to relax.

Health

Look after your throat! This is the area traditionally ruled by Taurus, so it may be your weak spot. When you feel run down you may develop a sore throat or a stiff neck. You may also go quite hoarse in times of great emotion. Your other main health concern is weight. Because you like taking life easy and you enjoy conducting a life-long love affair with food, the results are all too easy to imagine – and to see. You put on weight quickly but find it difficult to lose it again, thanks to your slow metabolism. Try to get plenty of fresh air and to combat what could be a sedentary job with lots of exercise in your spare time. Something energetic like aerobics may not appeal, but you'll enjoy dancing or taking brisk walks through the countryside.

Career

Hard work holds no terrors for you. In fact, you're a good, reliable member of any team. Because you find it unsettling not having a steady income you may avoid being self-employed, and will prefer being in a job that pays you regular amounts of money. Your natural affinity with money means that any career connected with finance, such as banking, insurance, financial consultancy or investments, is right up your street.

Other careers for which you're admirably suited include the beauty industry – you can excel at this because a typical Taurean is a walking advert for beauty preparations (Taurus is one of the best-looking signs in the zodiac). You can do well in professions connected with nature and the outdoors, such as farming, gardening and floristry. There are many Taureans in the music industry too, especially singers.

MERCURY AND YOUR COMMUNICATIONS

Where would we be without Mercury? This tiny planet rules everything connected with our communications, from the way we speak to the way we get about. The position of Mercury in your birth chart describes how fast or how slow you absorb information, the sorts of things you talk about, the way you communicate with other people and how much nervous energy you have.

Mercury is an important part of everyone's birth chart, but it has extra meaning for Geminis and Virgos because both these signs are ruled by Mercury.

Mercury is the closest planet to the Sun in the solar system, and its orbit lies between the Earth and the Sun. In fact, it is never more than 28 degrees away from the Sun. Mercury is one of the smallest known planets in the solar system, but it makes up in speed what it lacks in size. It whizzes around the Sun at about 108,000 miles an hour, to avoid being sucked into the Sun's fiery mass.

If you've always wondered how astrology works, here's a brief explanation. Your horoscope (a map of the planets' positions at the time of your birth) is divided up into twelve sections, known as 'houses'. Each one represents a different area of your life, and together they cover every aspect of our experiences on Earth. As Mercury moves around the heavens each year it progresses through each house in turn, affecting a particular part of your life, such as your health or career. If you plot its progress through your own chart, you'll be able to make the most of Mercury's influence in 2000. That way, you'll know when it's best to make contact with others and when it's wisest to keep your thoughts to yourself.

Mercury takes just over one year to complete its orbit of the Earth, but during this time it doesn't always travel forwards, it also appears to go backwards. When this happens, it means that, from our vantage point on Earth, Mercury has slowed down to such an extent that it seems to be backtracking through the skies. We call this retrograde motion. When Mercury is travelling forwards, we call it direct motion.

All the planets, with the exception of the Sun and Moon, go retrograde at some point during their orbit of the Earth. A retrograde Mercury is very important because it means that during this time our communications can hit delays and snags. Messages may go missing, letters could get lost in the post, appliances and gadgets can go on the blink. You may also find it hard to make yourself understood. In 2000, there are several periods when Mercury goes retrograde. These are between 21 February and 14 March, 23 June and 17 July, and between 18 October and 8 November. These are all times to keep a close eye on your communications. You may also feel happiest if you can avoid signing important agreements or contracts during these times.

To plot the progress of Mercury, fill in the blank diagram on page 9, writing '1' in the section next to your Sun sign, then numbering consecutively in an anti-clockwise direction around the signs until you have completed them all. It will now be easy to chart Mercury's movements. When it is in the same sign as your Sun, Mercury is in your first house, when he moves into the next sign (assuming he's not going retrograde) he occupies your second house, and so on, until he reaches your twelfth house, at which point he will move back into your first house again.

Diagram 1

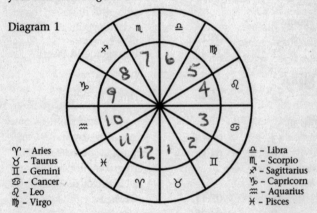

♈ – Aries
♉ – Taurus
♊ – Gemini
♋ – Cancer
♌ – Leo
♍ – Virgo

♎ – Libra
♏ – Scorpio
♐ – Sagittarius
♑ – Capricorn
♒ – Aquarius
♓ – Pisces

Here are the houses of the horoscope, numbered from one to twelve, for someone born with the Sun in Aquarius.

Diagram 2

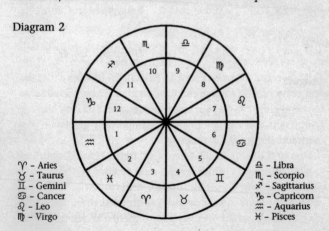

♈ – Aries
♉ – Taurus
♊ – Gemini
♋ – Cancer
♌ – Leo
♍ – Virgo

♎ – Libra
♏ – Scorpio
♐ – Sagittarius
♑ – Capricorn
♒ – Aquarius
♓ – Pisces

MERCURY'S ENTRY INTO THE SIGNS IN 2000
(All times are given in GMT, using the 24-hour clock)

January

Mercury is in Capricorn when 2000 begins

18	22:21	Aquarius

February

5	08:10	Pisces
21	12:47	Retrograde in Pisces

March

14	20:40	Direct in Pisces

April

13	00:18	Aries
30	03:54	Taurus

May

14	07:11	Gemini
30	04:28	Cancer

June

23	08:33	Retrograde in Cancer

July

17	13:21	Direct in Cancer

August

7	05:43	Leo
22	10:12	Virgo

September

7	21:23	Libra
28	13:29	Scorpio

October

18	13:42	Retrograde in Scorpio

November

7	07:29	Retrograde into Libra
8	02:29	Direct in Libra
8	21:43	Scorpio

December

3	20:27	Sagittarius
23	02:04	Capricorn

As 2000 begins, Mercury is moving through the final degrees of Capricorn, so it is in whichever house corresponds with the sign of Capricorn in your diagram. For instance, if you're an Aquarian, Mercury will move into your own sign at 22:21 GMT on 18 January and will occupy your first house. You can then read the explanation below telling you what to expect at this time. Mercury next moves signs at 08:10 GMT on 5 February, when he moves into Pisces. So if you're an Aquarian, Mercury will now be in your second house.

Mercury in the First House

This is a very busy time for you and you're completely wrapped up in your own ideas and concerns. Even if you aren't usually very chatty, you certainly are at the moment. However, you will much prefer talking about yourself to listening to other people! You've got lots of nervous energy at the moment and you'll enjoy getting out and about as much as possible. Look for ways of burning off excess energy, such as going for brisk walks or doing things that require initiative. This is a great opportunity to think about ways of pushing forward with ideas and getting new projects off the ground.

Mercury in the Second House

This is a great time to think about things that mean a lot to you. These might be beliefs, philosophies or anything else that gives meaning to your life. It's also a good time to consider the people that make your world go round. Do you devote enough time to them? You should also spare a thought for your finances, because this is a perfect opportunity to scrutinize them and make sure everything is in order. You could get in touch with someone who can give you some financial advice, or you might do some research into how to put your money to good use.

Mercury in the Third House

Chatty? You bet! This is probably when you're at your most talkative, and you'll enjoy nattering away about whatever pops into your head. You'll love talking to whoever happens to be around, but you'll get on especially well with neighbours, people you see in the course of your daily routine and close relatives. You'll soon start to feel restless if you have to spend too long in one place, so grab every opportunity to vary your schedule. You'll love taking off on day trips, going away for weekend breaks or simply abandoning your usual routine and doing something completely different. Communications will go well and you'll love playing with gadgets and appliances.

Mercury in the Fourth House

Your thoughts are never far away from your home and family life at the moment. You may be thinking about ways of improving your living standards and you could talk to people who can give you some advice. You're also wrapped up in thoughts of the past, and you may even be assailed by memories of far-off events or things you haven't thought about in ages. Pay attention to your dreams because they could give you some invaluable insights into the way you're feeling. Watch out for a slight tendency to be defensive or to imagine that people are trying to get at you. It's a lovely time for getting in touch with your nearest and dearest who live a long way away.

Mercury in the Fifth House

You'll really enjoy putting your mind to good use at the moment, especially if you do things that are based on fun. For instance, you might get engrossed in competitions, jigsaw puzzles, crosswords and quizzes, especially if there's the chance of winning a prize! Children and pets will be terrific company and you'll love romping with them. However, you may find that they're a lot more playful than usual. You may even be on the receiving end of some practical jokes. It's a super time to go on holiday, particularly if you're visiting somewhere you've never been before. Your social life promises to keep you busy and you'll find it easy to talk to loved ones about things that matter to you.

Mercury in the Sixth House

This is the ideal time of year to think about your health and well-being. Are you looking after yourself properly? If you've been battling with some strange symptoms, this is the perfect opportunity to get them investigated so you can put your mind at rest. You'll enjoy reading about medical matters, such as immersing yourself in a book that tells you how to keep fit or extolling the virtues of a specific eating plan. Your work might also keep you busy. Colleagues and customers will be chatty, and you could spend a lot of time dealing with paperwork or tapping away on the computer. It's a great time to look for a new job, especially if that means scanning the newspaper adverts, joining an employment agency or writing lots of application letters.

Mercury in the Seventh House

Communications play an important role in all your relationships at the moment. This is your chance to put across your point of view and to keep other people posted about what you think. You may enjoy having lots of chats with partners or you might have something important to discuss. Either way, the key to success is to keep talking! You're prepared to reach a compromise, so it's a marvellous time to get involved in negotiations and discussions. You'll also find that two heads are better than one right now, so it's the ideal time to do some teamwork. You'll enjoy bouncing your ideas off other people and listening to what they have to say.

Mercury in the Eighth House

It's time to turn your attention to your shared resources and official money matters. So if you share a bank account with your partner, you should check that everything is running smoothly. You might even decide to open a new account that suits you better or that pays a higher rate of interest. Speaking of accounts, this is an excellent time to fill in your tax return or complete your accounts for the year because you're in the right frame of mind for such things. This is also a good time to think about your close relationships. Do they bring you the emotional satisfaction that you need or is something missing? If you think there's room for improvement, talk to your partner about how to make things better between you.

Mercury in the Ninth House

The more you can expand your mental and physical horizons now, the happier you'll be. It's a time of year when you're filled with intellectual curiosity about the world and you long to cram your head with all sorts of facts and figures. You might decide to do some studying, whether you do it on a very informal basis or enrol for an evening class or college course. You'll certainly enjoy browsing around bookshops and library shelves, looking for books on your favourite subjects. Travel will appeal to you too, especially if you can visit somewhere exotic or a place that you've never been to before. You might become interested in a different religion from your own or you could be engrossed in something connected with philosophy, history or spirituality.

Mercury in the Tenth House

Spend some time thinking about your career prospects. Are you happy with the way things are going or does your professional life need a rethink? This is a great opportunity to talk to people who can give you some good advice. It's also an excellent time to share your ideas with your boss or a superior, especially if you're hoping to impress them. You could hear about a promotion or some improved job prospects, or you might decide to apply for a completely new job. It's also a marvellous opportunity to increase your qualifications, perhaps by training for something new or brushing up on an existing skill. You'll find it easier than usual to talk to older friends and relatives, especially if they can sometimes be a little tricky or hard to please.

Mercury in the Eleventh House

This is a great time to enjoy the company of friends and acquaintances. You'll love talking to them, especially if you can chat about subjects that make you think or that have humanitarian overtones. All sorts of intellectual activities will appeal to you at the moment. If your social circle is getting smaller and smaller, grab this chance to widen your horizons by meeting people who are on the same wavelength as you. For instance, you might decide to join a new club or society that caters for one of your interests. It's also a good opportunity to think about your hopes and wishes for the future. Are they going according to plan, or should you revise your strategy or even start again from scratch?

Mercury in the Twelfth House

You're entering a very reflective and reclusive period when you want to retreat from the madding crowd and have some time to yourself. You might enjoy taking the phone off the hook and curling up with a good book, or you could spend time studying subjects by yourself. There will be times when you feel quite tongue-tied, and you'll find it difficult to say exactly what you mean. You may even want to maintain a discreet silence on certain subjects, but make sure that other people don't take advantage of this by putting words into your mouth. You could be the recipient of someone's confidences, in which case you'll be a sympathetic listener. If you want to tell someone your secrets, choose your confidante wisely.

LOVE AND THE STARS

Love makes the world go round. When we know we're loved, we walk on air. We feel confident, happy and joyous. Without love, we feel miserable, lonely and as if life isn't worth living. If you're still looking for your perfect partner, this is the ideal guide for you. It will tell you which Sun signs you get on best with and which ones aren't such easy-going mates. By the way, there is hope for every astrological combination, and none are out and out disasters. It's simply that you'll find it easier to get on well with some signs than with others.

At the end of this section you'll see two compatibility charts – one showing how you get on in the love and sex stakes, and the other one telling you which signs make the best friends. These charts will instantly remind you which signs get on best and which struggle to keep the peace. Each combination has been given marks out of ten, with ten points being a fabulous pairing and one point being pretty grim. Find the woman's Sun sign along the top line of the chart, then look down the left-hand column for the man's sign. The square where these two lines meet will give you the result of this astrological combination. For instance, when assessing the love and sex compatibility of a Leo woman and a Cancerian man, they score six out of ten.

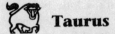

Taurus

Taureans are literally in their element when they're with Virgos or Capricorns who, like themselves, are Earth signs. Two Taureans will get along very happily together, although they could become so wedded to routine that they get stuck in a rut. They may also encourage one another to eat too much. A Taurean will enjoy being with a Virgo, because they respect the Virgo's methodical nature. They'll also like encouraging their Virgo to relax and take life easy. Money will form a link between a Taurean and a Capricorn, with plenty of serious discussions on how to make it and what to do with it once they've got it. There will also be a strong sexual rapport, and the Taurean will encourage the more sensual side of the Capricorn.

The relationship between a Taurean and members of the Water element is also very good. A Taurean and a Cancerian will revel in one another's company and will probably be so happy at home that they'll rarely stir from their armchairs. They both have a strong need for emotional security and will stick together through thick and thin. There's plenty of passion when a Taurean pairs up with a Scorpio, although the faithful Taurean could become fed up with the Scorpio's jealous nature. They simply won't understand what they're being accused of, and their loyal nature will be offended by the very thought that they could be a two-timer. A Taurean will be delighted by a delicate Piscean, and will want to take care of such a vulnerable and sensitive creature.

Things become rather more complicated when a Taurean pairs up with an Arien, Leo or Sagittarian, all of whom are Fire signs. They have very little in common – Taureans like to take things slowly while Fire signs want to make things happen *now*. It's particularly difficult between a Taurean and an Arien – the careful Taurean will feel harried and rushed by the impetuous Arien. It's a little better when a Taurean gets together with a Leo, because they share a deep appreciation of the good things in life, although the Taurean will be horrified by the Leo's ability to spend money. Making joint decisions could be difficult, however, because they'll both stand their ground and refuse to budge. A Taurean and a Sagittarian simply don't understand each other – they're on such different wavelengths. Any Taurean displays of possessiveness will make the independent Sagittarian want to run a mile.

Taureans are equally mystified by the Air signs – Gemini, Libra and Aquarius. What they see as the flightiness of Gemini drives them barmy – why can't the Gemini settle down and do one thing at a time? The Taurean will probably feel quite exhausted by the Gemini's many interests and bubbly character. Taurus and Libra are a surprisingly good pairing, because they share a need for beauty, luxury and love. This could end up costing the penny-wise Taurean quite a packet, but they'll have a deliciously romantic time along the way. Taurus and Aquarius are chalk and cheese, and neither one is prepared to meet the other one halfway. The Taurean need to keep tabs on their loved one's every movement will irritate the freedom-loving Aquarian, and there will be plenty of rows as a result.

Gemini

One of the Air signs, Geminis get on very well with their fellow members of this element – Librans and Aquarians. Two Geminis are the astrological equivalent of double trouble – they chat nineteen to the dozen and revel in the company of someone who understands them so well. A Gemini delights in being with a Libran, because they enjoy the intellectual company and will benefit from the Libran's (usually) relaxed approach to life. They'll also learn to deal with their emotions more if a sympathetic Libran can guide them. Gemini and Aquarius is a very exciting pairing – the Gemini is encouraged to think deeply and knows that the Aquarian won't put up with any woolly ideas or fudged arguments.

Geminis also get on well with the three Fire signs – Aries, Leo and Sagittarius. A Gemini loves being with a racy, adventurous Arien, and together they enjoy keeping abreast of all the latest gossip and cultural developments. However, after the first flush of enthusiasm has worn off, the Gemini may find the Arien's strong need for sex rather hard to take. The Gemini gets on very well with a Leo. They delight in the Leo's affectionate nature and are amused by their need to have the best that money can buy – and they'll gladly share in the spoils. Gemini and Sagittarius are an excellent combination, because they sit opposite each other in the zodiac and so complement one another's character. The Gemini will be fascinated by the erudite and knowledgeable Sagittarian.

Gemini doesn't do so well with the Earth signs of Taurus and Capricorn, although they get on better with Virgo. The Gemini finds it difficult to understand a Taurean, because they see the world from such different viewpoints. The Gemini takes a more light-hearted approach and lives life at such a speed that they find it difficult to slow down to the more measured pace of a Taurean. The wonderfully dry Capricorn sense of humour is a source of constant delight to a Gemini. However, they're less taken with the Capricorn's streak of pessimism and their love of tradition. Of the three Earth signs, Gemini and Virgo are the most compatible. The Gemini shares the Virgo's brainpower and they have long, fascinating conversations.

When a Gemini gets together with the Water signs, the result can be enjoyable or puzzling. Gemini and Cancer have little in common, because the Gemini wants to spread their emotional and intellectual wings, whereas a Cancerian likes to stay close to home and has little interest in abstract ideas. Gemini finds Scorpio perplexing because they operate on such different levels. A Gemini tends to skim along the surface of things, so often deals with life on a superficial level, whereas a Scorpio likes to dig deep and has to have an emotional investment in everything they do. A Gemini appreciates the subtlety and sensitivity of a Piscean, but they're likely to make off-the-cuff comments that unwittingly hurt the Piscean.

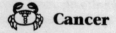 **Cancer**

Cancerians revel in the company of their fellow Water signs of Scorpio and Pisces. When two Cancerians get together they could spend most of their time at home or eating – preferably both. They feel safe in the knowledge that they both have a strong need for love, but their innate Cancerian tenacity may mean they cling on to the relationship even if it's long past its best. A Cancerian is enchanted with a Scorpio, because at last they feel free to really let rip emotionally. However, the intuitive Cancerian should beware of soaking up the Scorpio's darker moods like a psychic sponge. A Cancerian will take one look at a delicate Piscean and want to invite them home for a good hot meal. All the Cancerian's protective instincts are aroused by a gentle Piscean, but their anger will also be aroused if it turns out the Piscean has been leading a double life behind their back.

Cancerians also find a great deal of comfort in the company of the Earth signs – Taurus, Virgo and Capricorn. Cancer and Taurus were made for each other – they both adore home comforts and they trust one another implicitly. The Cancerian loves making a cosy nest for their hard-working Taurean. A Cancerian finds a Virgo a more difficult proposition, especially emotionally. Whereas Cancer is all warm hugs and holding hands by the fire, Virgo prefers to read a book and reserve any displays of affection for the bedroom. Cancer and Capricorn are opposite numbers in the zodiac, so share a tremendous rapport. They also share the same values of home, tradition and family, and if anyone can help a Capricorn to relax and take life easy, it's a Cancerian.

Life becomes more difficult when it comes to a Cancerian's relationship with any of the Air signs. They simply don't understand one another. A Cancerian can't make a Gemini out. They feel confused by what they think of as the Gemini's flightiness and inability to stay in one place for long. They can also be easily hurt by the Gemini's difficulty in expressing their emotions. A Cancerian gets on much better with a Libran. They're both ambitious in their own ways and so have a great deal in common. The Cancerian enjoys the Libran's romantic nature, but the Cancerian tendency to cling doesn't go down well. A Cancerian regards a typical Aquarian as a being from another planet. They're hurt by the Aquarian's strong need for independence and dislike of having to account for their every action, and are dismayed and confused by the Aquarian's hot-and-cold attitude to sex.

The Fire signs of Aries, Leo and Sagittarius are also a potential source of bewilderment to the gentle Cancerian. They understand the drive and ambition of an Arien, but will be stung by their blunt speech and worried about their daredevil tendencies. What if they hurt themselves? A Cancerian gets on well with a Leo because they share a strong love of family and are both openly affectionate and loving. The Cancerian enjoys creating a home that the Leo can feel proud of. So far, so good, but the story isn't so simple when a Cancerian pairs up with a Sagittarian. They're too different to understand one another – the Cancerian wants to stay at home with the family while the Sagittarian has an instinctive need to roam the world. As a result, the Cancerian will be disappointed, and then hurt, when the Sagittarian's busy schedule takes them away from home too often.

 Leo

Leos adore the company of their fellow Fire signs, Ariens and Sagittarius. They understand one another and enjoy each other's spontaneous warmth and affection. A Leo is amused by the exuberance and impulsiveness of an Arien, and they enjoy being persuaded to let their hair down a bit and not worry too much about appearances. A Leo enjoys the dash and vitality of a Sagittarian, although they may feel irritated if they can never get hold of them on the phone or the Sagittarian is always off doing other things. Two Leos together either love or loathe one another. One of them should be prepared to take a back seat, otherwise they'll both be vying for the limelight all the time.

The three Air signs of Gemini, Libra and Aquarius all get on well with Leos. When a Leo pairs up with a Gemini, you can expect lots of laughter and plenty of fascinating conversations. The demonstrative Leo is able to help the Gemini be more openly affectionate and loving. Leo and Libra is a great combination, and the Leo is enchanted by the Libran's fair-minded attitude. Both signs love luxury and all the good things in life but their bank managers may not be so pleased by the amount of the money they manage to spend. Leo and Aquarius sit opposite one another across the horoscope, so they already have a great deal in common. They're fascinated by one another but they're both very stubborn, so any disputes between them usually end in stalemate because neither is prepared to concede any ground.

Leos don't really understand the Earth signs. Although Leos admire their practical approach to life, they find it rather restricting. A Leo enjoys the sensuous and hedonistic side of a Taurean's character but may become frustrated by their fear of change. Leo and Virgo have very little in common, especially when it comes to food – the Leo wants to tuck in at all the best restaurants while the Virgo is worried about the state of the kitchens, the number of calories and the size of the bill. A Leo respects the Capricorn's desire to support their family and approves of their need to be seen in the best possible light, but they feel hurt by the Capricorn's difficulty in showing their feelings.

When a Leo gets together with one of the Water signs – Cancer, Scorpio or Pisces – they'll enjoy the sexual side of the relationship but could eventually feel stifled by all that Watery emotion. A Leo and a Cancerian adore making a home together and both dote on their children. The Leo also likes comforting their vulnerable Cancerian – provided this doesn't happen too often. A Leo and a Scorpio will be powerfully attracted to one another, but power could also pull them apart – who's going to wear the trousers? They'll also lock horns during rows and both of them will refuse to back down. A Leo delights in a sophisticated Piscean, but may become irritated by their indecision and jangly nerves.

💇 Virgo

As you might imagine, Virgos are happy with their fellow Earth signs of Taurus and Capricorn because they share the same practical attitude. A Virgo enjoys the steady, reassuring company of a Taurean, and they might even learn to relax a little instead of worrying themselves into the ground over the slightest problem. When two Virgos get together it can be too much of a good thing. Although at first they'll love talking to someone who shares so many of their preoccupations and ideas, they can soon drive one another round the bend. When a Virgo first meets a Capricorn they're delighted to know someone who's obviously got their head screwed on. It's only later on that they wish the Capricorn could lighten up every now and then.

Virgos get on well with Cancerians, Scorpios and Pisceans, the three Water signs. A Virgo enjoys being looked after by a considerate Cancerian, although they'll worry about their waistline and may get irritated by the Cancerian's super-sensitive feelings. You can expect plenty of long, analytical conversations when a Virgo gets together with a Scorpio. They both love getting to the bottom of subjects and will endlessly talk things through. They'll also get on extremely well in the bedroom. Pisces is Virgo's opposite sign, but although some opposites thrive in each other's company, that isn't always the case with this combination. The Virgo could soon grow impatient with the dreamy Piscean and will long to tell them a few home truths.

Although the other Earth signs don't usually get on well with Air signs, it's different for Virgos. They understand the intellectual energies of Geminis, Librans and Aquarians. A Virgo thrives in a Gemini's company, and they spend hours chatting over the phone if they can't get together in person. It's difficult for them to discuss their emotions, however, and they may never tell each other how they really feel. A Virgo admires a sophisticated, charming Libran, and marvels at their diplomacy. How do they do it? Expect a few sparks to fly when a Virgo pairs up with an Aquarian, because both of them have very strong opinions and aren't afraid to air them. The result is a lot of hot air and some vigorous arguments.

The three Fire signs – Aries, Leo and Sagittarius – are a source of endless fascination to a Virgo. They've got so much energy! A Virgo finds an Arien exciting but their relationship could be short-lived because the Virgo will be so irritated by the Arien's devil-may-care attitude to life. When a Virgo pairs up with a

Leo, they'll be intrigued by this person's comparatively lavish lifestyle but their own modest temperament will be shocked if the Leo enjoys showing off. A Virgo is able to talk to a Sagittarius until the cows come home – they're both fascinated by ideas, although the precise Virgo will first be amused, and then irritated, by the Sagittarian's rather relaxed attitude to hard facts.

 Libra

Of all the members of the zodiac, this is the one that finds it easiest to get on with the other signs. Librans get on particularly well with Geminis and Aquarians, their fellow Air signs. A Libran is enchanted by a Gemini's quick brain and ready wit, and they enjoy endless discussions on all sorts of subjects. When two Librans get together, they revel in the resulting harmonious atmosphere but it's almost impossible for them to reach any decisions – each one defers to the other while being unable to say what they really want. A Libran is intrigued by the independence and sharp mind of an Aquarian, but their feelings could be hurt by the Aquarian's emotional coolness.

Libra enjoys being with the three Fire signs – Aries, Leo and Sagittarius. Libra, who often takes life at rather a slow pace, is energized by a lively Arien, and they complement one another's personalities well. However, the Libran may occasionally feel hurt by the Arien's single-mindedness and blunt speech. A Libran adores the luxury-loving ways of a Leo, and they'll both spend a fortune in the pursuit of happiness. They also get on well in the bedroom. When a Libran gets together with an exuberant Sagittarian, they'll have great fun. All the same, the Sagittarian need for honesty could fluster the Libran, who adopts a much more diplomatic approach to life.

Although the other two Air signs can find it hard to understand members of the Water element, it's different for Librans. They're more sympathetic to the emotional energies of Cancerians, Scorpios and Pisceans. A Libran delights in the protective care of a Cancerian, but those ever-changing Cancerians moods may be hard for a balanced Libran to take. Those deep Scorpio emotions will intrigue the Libran but they may quickly become bogged down by such an intense outlook on life and will be desperate for some light relief. As for Pisces, the Libran is charmed by the Piscean's delicate nature and creative gifts, but both signs hate facing up to unpleasant facts so this couple may never deal with any problems that lie between them.

Libra enjoys the reliable natures of Taurus, Virgo and Capricorn, the Earth signs. A Libran appreciates the company of a relaxed and easy-going Taurean, although they may sometimes regret the Taurean's lack of imagination. When a Libran and a Virgo get together, the Libran enjoys the Virgo's mental abilities but their critical comments will soon cut the Libran to the quick. The Libran may not come back for a second tongue-lashing. A Libran understands the ambitions of a Capricorn, and likes their steady nature and the way they support their family. However, there could soon be rows about money, with the Libran spending a lot more than the Capricorn thinks is necessary.

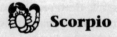 **Scorpio**

Not every sign gets on well with its fellow members, yet an astonishing number of Scorpios pair up. They feel safe together because they know the worst and best about each other. When things are good, they're brilliant but these two can also bring out the worst in each other, with intense silences and brooding sulks. A Scorpio enjoys the tender ministrations of a loving Cancerian, and adores being with someone who's so obviously concerned about their welfare. Feelings run deep when a Scorpio pairs up with a Piscean, although the Scorpio may become impatient with the Piscean's reluctance to face up to unpalatable truths.

The three Earth signs, Taurus, Virgo and Capricorn, are well-suited to the Scorpio temperament. Those astrological opposites, Scorpio and Taurus, enjoy a powerful relationship, much of which probably takes place in the bedroom, but whenever they have a disagreement there's an atmosphere you could cut with a knife, and neither of them will be prepared to admit they were in the wrong. A Scorpio is attracted to a neat, analytical Virgo but their feelings will be hurt by this sign's tendency to criticize. What's more, their pride stops them telling the Virgo how they feel. The Scorpio admires a practical Capricorn, especially if they've earned a lot of respect through their work, but this could be a rather chilly pairing because both signs find it difficult to show their feelings.

When you put a Scorpio together with one of the three Fire signs, they'll either get on famously or won't understand one another at all. A Scorpio revels in the lusty Arien's sex drive, although they'll soon feel tired if they try to keep up with the Arien's busy schedule. The combination of Scorpio and Leo packs quite a punch. They're both very strong personalities, but they boss one another around like mad and find it almost impossible to achieve a compromise if they fall out. A Scorpio likes to take life at a measured pace, so they're bemused by a Sagittarian's need to keep busy all the time. In the end, they'll become fed up with never seeing the Sagittarian, or playing second fiddle to all their other interests.

Scorpio is bemused by the three Air signs – Gemini, Libran and Aquarius – because they operate on such completely different wavelengths. A Scorpio can be good friends with a Gemini but they're at emotional cross-purposes, with the Scorpio's intense approach to life too much for a light-hearted

Gemini to cope with. Emotions are also the bugbear between a Scorpio and a Libran. Everything is great at first, but the Scorpio's powerful feelings and dark moods will eventually send the Libran running in the opposite direction. You can expect some tense arguments when a Scorpio pairs up with an Aquarian – they're both convinced that they're right and the other one is wrong.

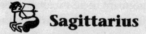 **Sagittarius**

When a Sagittarian pairs up with a fellow Fire sign, there's plenty of warmth and the odd firework. A Sagittarian is thrilled by the adventurous spirit of an Arien, and they love exploring the world together. There are plenty of tall tales when a Sagittarian gets together with a Leo – they'll try to outdo each other, dropping names and recounting their greatest triumphs. If the Leo is slightly pompous, the Sagittarian is able to take them down a peg or two, but they must beware of hurting the Leo's feelings. As for two Sagittarians, they'll spur each other on and encourage one another to gain as much experience of life as possible. You probably won't be able to move in their house for books.

With their endless curiosity about the world, Sagittarians understand the intellectual Air signs very well. A Sagittarian enjoys the chatty company of a Gemini and, because they're opposite numbers in the zodiac, the Sagittarian is able to encourage the Gemini to see things through and explore them in more detail than usual. A refined and diplomatic Libran will try to teach the blunt Sagittarian not to say the first thing that pops into their head. However, the Sagittarian may eventually find the Libran's sense of balance rather trying – why can't they get more worked up about things? There's plenty of straight talking when a Sagittarian teams up with an

Aquarian – they both have a high regard for honesty. The independent Sagittarian respects the Aquarian's need for freedom, but may feel rather stung by their periods of emotional coolness.

A Sagittarian will struggle to understand the Earth signs. They respect the Taurean's ability to work hard but they're driven to distraction by their reluctance to make changes and break out of any ruts they've fallen into. A Sagittarian enjoys talking to a brainy Virgo, but their expansive and spontaneous nature could eventually be restricted by the Virgo's need to think things through before taking action. When a Sagittarian gets together with a Capricorn, it's a case of optimism versus pessimism. While the Sagittarian's glass is half-full, the Capricorn's is always half-empty, and this causes many rows and possibly some ill feeling.

There could be lots of misunderstandings when a Sagittarian gets involved with one of the Water signs. A Sagittarian needs a bigger social circle than their family, whereas a Cancerian is quite happy surrounded by kith and kin. The Sagittarian need for independence won't go down well, either. It's like oil and water when a Sagittarian pairs up with a Scorpio. The Sagittarian is the roamer of the zodiac, whereas the Scorpio wants them where they can see them, in case they're up to no good. All will be well if the Sagittarian gets together with a strong-minded Piscean. In fact, they'll really enjoy one another's company. A Piscean who's lost in a world of their own, however, will soon leave them cold.

 **Capricorn**

Despite their outward poise, a Capricorn is very easily hurt so they need to know their feelings won't be trampled on. There's least danger of that when they get together with a fellow Earth sign. A Capricorn adores a Taurean's deep sense of responsibility and they'll both work hard to create their ideal home. A Capricorn appreciates the methodical approach of a Virgo, but could feel deeply hurt by the Virgo's sharp tongue and caustic remarks. If two Capricorns team up, one of them must be demonstrative and openly affectionate, otherwise the relationship could be rather sterile and serious.

Capricorns also feel safe with members of the Water signs. When a Capricorn gets together with a Cancerian, they do their utmost to make their home a haven. They'll get great satisfaction from channelling their energies into bringing up a family. A Capricorn may be rather bemused by the depth and intensity of a Scorpio's emotions – Capricorns are too reserved to indulge in such drama themselves and it can make them feel uncomfortable. A no-nonsense Capricorn could be perplexed by an extremely vulnerable Piscean and won't know how to handle them. Should they give them a hanky or tell them to pull themselves together?

The Air signs can also make a Capricorn feel somewhat unsettled. They're fascinated by a Gemini's breadth of knowledge and endless chat, but they also find them superficial and rather flighty. In fact, the Capricorn probably doesn't trust the Gemini. A Capricorn feels far happier in the company of a Libran. Here's someone who seems much steadier emotionally and who can help the Capricorn to unwind after a hard day's work. It can be great or ghastly when a Capricorn sets their sights on an Aquarian. They understand each other provided the Aquarian isn't too unconventional, but the Capricorn feels uncomfortable and embarrassed by any displays of eccentricity, deliberate or not.

The Fire signs help to warm up the Capricorn, who can be rather remote and distant at times. A Capricorn admires the Arien's drive and initiative, but endlessly tells them to look before they leap and could become irritated when they don't take this sage advice. When a Capricorn gets together with a

Leo, they won't need to worry about appearances – the Capricorn will feel justly proud of the smart Leo. However, they could wince when the bills come in and they discover how much those clothes cost. A Capricorn thinks a Sagittarian must have come from another planet – how can they be so relaxed and laid-back all the time? They have great respect for the Sagittarian's wisdom and philosophy, but they quickly become fed up with having to fit in around the Sagittarian's hectic social life.

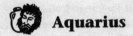 **Aquarius**

Put an Aquarian with a fellow Air sign and they're happy. They thoroughly enjoy being with a lively Gemini and love discussing everything under the sun with them. They may not have a very exciting sex life, but their mental closeness will more than make up for it. The gentle charms of a Libran calms down an Aquarian when their nerves become frayed, although they disapprove of the Libran's innate tact and diplomacy – why can't they just say what they think, instead of sitting on the fence? With two Aquarians you never know what to expect, other than that they'll be great friends. They'll certainly do a lot of talking, but could spend more time debating esoteric ideas and abstract concepts.

An Aquarian likes all the Fire signs, although they find Ariens hard to fathom and can become exhausted by an Arien's endless supply of energy and enthusiasm. There are no such problems when an Aquarian pairs up with a Leo because they complement each other in many ways. The Aquarian teaches objectivity to the Leo, who in return encourages the Aquarian to express their emotions more. An Aquarian thoroughly enjoys being with a Sagittarian because both of them hate being tied down. As a result, they respect one another's independence and will probably rarely see each other because of all their spare-time activities.

It's not quite so simple when an Aquarian joins forces with one of the Earth signs. An Aquarian will lock horns with a Taurean sooner or later, because neither of them is able to back down once a disagreement has started. The Aquarian will also feel very restricted by the Taurean's possessiveness. The Virgo's analytical approach to life intrigues the Aquarian but they'll sit up all night arguing the toss over everything, with each one convinced that they've got all the answers. When an Aquarian meets a Capricorn, they've got their work cut out for them if they're to find a happy medium between the erratic Aquarian and the conventional Capricorn.

An Aquarian feels out of their depth when they're with one of the Water signs. They simply don't understand what makes a Cancerian tick – why do they worry themselves sick over things that they can't change? The Aquarian finds it all most peculiar. They also find it difficult to understand a Scorpio who takes so many things so seriously. Although the Aquarian also has a list of topics that mean a lot to them, they're not the sort of things that hold the slightest interest for a Scorpio. It's more or less the same story with a Pisces, because their huge resources of emotion make the Aquarian feel uncomfortable and fill them with a strong desire to escape as fast as possible.

 **Pisces**

Relationships mean a lot to a sensitive Piscean, but they're easily misunderstood by many of the more robust signs. There are no such worries with the other Water signs, however. A Piscean loves being with a tender Cancerian who knows how to help them relax and feel safe. They really enjoy playing house together but the emotional scenes will blow the roof off.

The relationship between a Piscean and a Scorpio can be quite spicy and sexy, but the Piscean is turned off if the Scorpio becomes too intense and dramatic. Two Pisceans feel safe with one another, but they'll push all their problems under the carpet unless one of them is more objective.

A Piscean also gets on well with the Earth signs, although with a few reservations. A Piscean takes comfort from being looked after by a protective Taurean, but after a while they could feel stifled by the Taurean's possessive and matter-of-fact attitude. The relationship between a Piscean and a Virgo starts off well but the Piscean could soon feel crushed by the Virgo's criticism and will need more emotional reassurance than the Virgo is able to give. A Piscean feels safe with a Capricorn because they're so dependable but in the end this may begin to bug them. It's not that they want the Capricorn to two-time them, more that they'd like a little unpredictability every now and then.

A Piscean is fascinated by the Air signs but their apparent lack of emotion could cause problems. A Piscean and a Gemini are terrific friends but could encounter difficulties as lovers. The Piscean's strong emotional needs are too much for the Gemini to handle – they'll feel as if they're drowning. The Piscean is on much firmer ground with a Libran, who'll go out of their way to keep the Piscean happy. Neither sign is good at facing up to any nasty truths, however. An Aquarian is too much for a sensitive Piscean, who views the world through rose-coloured specs. An Aquarian, on the other hand, has uncomfortably clear vision.

The Fire signs can cheer up a Piscean enormously, but any prolonged displays of emotion will make the Fire signs feel weighed down. The Piscean is fascinated by an Arien's exploits but could feel reluctant to join in. They'll also be easily hurt by some of the Arien's off-the-cuff remarks. When a Piscean pairs up with a Leo they appreciate the way the Leo wants to take charge and look after them. After a while, however, this could grate on them and they'll want to be more independent. A Piscean enjoys discussing philosophy and spiritual ideas with a Sagittarian – they can sit up half the night talking things through. The Sagittarian brand of honesty could hurt the Piscean at times, but they know this isn't malicious and will quickly forgive such outbursts.

Aries

Because Ariens belong to the Fire element, they get on very well with their fellow Fire signs Leo and Sagittarius. All the same, an Arien getting together with a Leo will soon notice a distinct drop in their bank balance, because they'll enjoy going to all the swankiest restaurants and sitting in the best seats at the theatre. When an Arien pairs up with a Sagittarian, they'll compete over who drives the fastest car and has the most exciting holidays. When two Ariens get together the results can be combustible. Ideally, one Arien should be a lot quieter, otherwise they'll spend most of their time jostling for power. All these combinations are very sexy and physical.

Ariens also thrive in the company of the three Air signs – Gemini, Libra and Aquarius. Of the three, they get on best with Geminis, who share their rather childlike view of the world and also their sense of fun. An Arien and a Gemini enjoy hatching all sorts of ideas and schemes, even if they never get round to putting them into action. There's an exciting sense of friction between Aries and Libra, their opposite number in the zodiac. An Arien will be enchanted by the way their Libran caters to their every need, but may become impatient when the Libran also wants to look after other people. An Arien will be captivated by the originality of an Aquarian, although at times they'll be driven mad by the Aquarian's eccentric approach to life and the way they blow hot and cold in the bedroom.

Ariens don't do so well with the Earth signs – Taurus, Virgo and Capricorn. The very careful, slightly plodding nature of a typical Taurean can drive an Arien barmy at times, and although they'll respect – and benefit from – the Taurean's practical approach to life, it can still fill them with irritation. An Arien finds it difficult to fathom a Virgo, because their attitudes to life are diametrically opposed. An Arien likes to jump in with both feet, while a Virgo prefers to take things slowly and analyse every possibility before committing themselves. An Arien can get on quite well with a Capricorn, because they're linked by their sense of ambition and their earthy sexual needs.

An Arien is out of their depth with any of the Water signs – Cancer, Scorpio and Pisces. They quickly become irritated by the defensive Cancerian, although they'll love their cooking. An Arien will enjoy a very passionate affair with a Scorpio, but the Scorpio's need to know exactly what the Arien is up to when their back is turned will soon cause problems and rifts. Although an Arien may begin a relationship with a Pisces by wanting to look after them and protect them from the harsh realities of life, eventually the Piscean's extremely sensitive nature may bring out the Arien's bullying streak.

Compatibility in Love and Sex at a glance

F / M	♈	♉	♊	♋	♌	♍	♎	♏	♐	♑	♒	♓
♈	8	5	9	7	9	4	7	8	9	7	7	3
♉	6	8	4	10	7	8	8	7	3	8	2	8
♊	8	2	7	3	8	7	9	4	9	4	9	4
♋	5	10	4	8	6	5	6	8	2	9	2	8
♌	9	8	9	7	7	4	9	6	8	7	9	6
♍	4	8	6	4	4	7	6	7	7	9	4	4
♎	7	8	10	7	8	5	9	6	9	6	10	6
♏	7	9	4	7	6	6	7	10	5	6	5	7
♐	9	4	10	4	9	7	8	4	9	6	9	5
♑	7	8	4	9	6	8	6	4	4	8	4	5
♒	8	6	9	4	9	4	9	6	8	7	8	2
♓	7	6	7	9	6	7	6	9	7	5	4	9

1 = the pits
10 = the peaks

Key

♈ – Aries
♉ – Taurus
♊ – Gemini
♋ – Cancer
♌ – Leo
♍ – Virgo

♎ – Libra
♏ – Scorpio
♐ – Sagittarius
♑ – Capricorn
♒ – Aquarius
♓ – Pisces

Compatibility in Friendship at a glance

F M	♈	♉	♊	♋	♌	♍	♎	♏	♐	♑	♒	♓
♈	8	5	10	5	9	3	7	8	9	6	8	5
♉	6	9	6	10	7	8	7	6	4	9	3	9
♊	9	3	9	4	9	8	10	5	10	5	10	6
♋	6	9	4	9	5	4	6	9	4	10	3	9
♌	10	7	9	6	9	4	8	6	9	6	9	7
♍	5	9	8	4	4	8	5	8	8	10	5	6
♎	8	9	10	8	8	6	9	5	9	6	10	7
♏	7	8	5	8	7	7	6	9	4	5	6	8
♐	9	5	10	4	10	8	8	4	10	7	9	6
♑	6	9	5	10	6	9	5	5	4	9	5	6
♒	9	6	10	5	9	5	9	7	9	5	9	3
♓	6	7	6	10	6	8	7	9	8	6	4	10

1 = the pits
10 = the peaks

Key

♈ – Aries
♉ – Taurus
♊ – Gemini
♋ – Cancer
♌ – Leo
♍ – Virgo

♎ – Libra
♏ – Scorpio
♐ – Sagittarius
♑ – Capricorn
♒ – Aquarius
♓ – Pisces

HOBBIES AND THE STARS

What do you do in your spare time? If you're looking for some new interests to keep you occupied in 2000, read on to discover which hobbies are ideal for your Sun sign.

 **Taurus**

You belong to one of the Earth signs, so it's no surprise that many Taureans were born with green fingers. You always feel better when you can be out in the fresh air, especially if you're in beautiful surroundings, so you adore gardening. Even if you're not keen on wielding a spade yourself you'll enjoy appreciating other people's efforts. Cooking is something that has enormous appeal for you and you enjoy creating gourmet meals, especially if the ingredients include your favourite foods. You also enjoy visiting swanky restaurants, although some of the gilt will be wiped off the gingerbread if you don't think you're getting value for money. Members of your sign are renowned for having beautiful voices so you might enjoy singing in a choir or on your own.

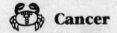 Gemini

One of your favourite ways of passing the time is to curl up with a good book. You'll eagerly read newspapers and magazines as well, and you always attempt crosswords and other sorts of puzzle even if you don't always finish them. Jigsaws intrigue you, especially if you can do something else at the same time, such as listening to music or watching the TV. You belong to a sign that doesn't like sitting still for long and you absolutely thrive on keeping active, so it's important for you to enjoy hobbies that make sure you get plenty of exercise. Tennis is a classic Gemini sport because it involves a lot of skill but it also boosts your social life. Dancing is another activity that helps you to keep fit while having a really good time.

Cancer

Home comforts are very important to you, so you spend a lot of time and money on making sure your home is the way you want it. You may enjoy reading magazines on interior design or you could be glued to all the DIY programmes on TV, adapting the best ideas for your own home. One of your greatest skills is cooking, because you belong to a sign that derives enormous emotional comfort from food. You take pleasure in cooking for your loved ones and you probably have a big collection of cookery books to provide you with endless inspiration. Water sports could appeal to you, especially if they involve visiting your favourite beach. You might also enjoy fishing, particularly if you can do it by moonlight.

Leo

You have a host of artistic skills and talents at your fingertips because you belong to the one of the most creative signs in the zodiac. One of your favourite hobbies is amateur dramatics, because most Leos adore being in the limelight. You may even have thought about becoming a professional actor because you enjoy treading the boards so much. You might also enjoy dancing, whether you go to regular classes or you simply love tripping the light fantastic with your partner. Travel appeals to you, especially if you can visit luxurious hotels in hot parts of the world. However, you're not very keen on roughing it! Clothes are very important to you, so you enjoy shopping for the latest fashions and you may also be an accomplished dressmaker.

 Virgo

One of your favourite pastimes is to keep up to date with your health. You're fascinated by medical matters and you enjoy reading books telling you how to keep fit. You may even try out all the latest eating regimes, hoping that you'll find one that suits you perfectly. This interest in health means you're keen to eat well, and you could enjoy growing your own vegetables. Even cultivating a few herbs in a windowbox will give you a sense of achievement and you'll be pleased to think they are doing you good. You have tremendous patience so you might enjoy fiddly hobbies that require great dexterity, such as knitting, needlepoint and sewing. You might also enjoy painting designs on china and glass.

Libra

Libra is a very sensual sign, so any hobbies that appeal to your senses are bound to go down well. You love delicious smells so you might enjoy learning about aromatherapy, so you can cure yourself of minor ailments and also create your own bath oils. You could also get a big thrill out of making your own cosmetics or soaps, and you might become so good at them that you give them away as gifts. You take great pride in looking good, so you enjoy visiting your favourite shops and keeping up with the latest fashions. Music is one of your great loves and you might play an instrument or sing. If not, you certainly appreciate other people's musical talents and you enjoy going to concerts and recitals.

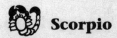 **Scorpio**

Whatever hobbies you choose, they have to mean a lot to you. You simply aren't interested in activities that don't carry an emotional meaning for you and you'd rather not bother with them at all. One pastime that's dear to the hearts of most Scorpios is wine-tasting. You might enjoy teaching yourself all about wine, either with the help of some good books or simply by drinking whatever appeals to you. You're fascinated by mysteries, and you could enjoy reading lots of whodunits or books on true crimes. You are also intrigued by things that go bump in the night, and you can't resist going on ghost hunts or visiting famous places that are known to be haunted.

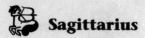 **Sagittarius**

You're one of the great collectors of the zodiac, whether you know it or not. You may not think that you collect anything at all, but other people will take one look at all your books and beg to disagree with you. Reading is one of your great pleasures in life and you're always buying books on your latest enthusiasms. Travel is something else that appeals to you, and you love planning where you're going to go next on holiday. You like to keep active and you enjoy outdoor sports in particular. Horse-riding is a classic Sagittarian activity, and you enjoy going to the races and having a little flutter. You also like activities that present you with a challenge – you're always determined to beat it!

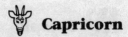 **Capricorn**

If you're a typical Capricorn you often take life rather seriously, so it's important for you to have lots of spare-time activities that allow you to relax. However, you've got to find the time first, and that means stopping work rather than burning the candle at both ends. Something that might appeal to you is rock-climbing, and you'll enjoy planning the strategy of how you're going to get to the top. Even a gentle walk amid mountain scenery does you a lot of good and helps you to relax. You're a very practical sign and you enjoy gardening. Not only does it help to ground you, you also like growing your own fruit and vegetables and then comparing the prices with those in the shops. Music helps you to unwind, and you'll love going to the opera or a glittering concert.

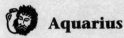 **Aquarius**

Most Aquarians have such a wide range of interests that almost anything is bound to appeal to you. You may go through phases, immersing yourself in one hobby for years until another one takes your fancy. However, you are only interested in activities that keep you intellectually stimulated and that teach you more about the world. You may go to lots of different evening classes, and you might even study for a degree in your spare time. Eastern philosophy could appeal, and you might also be an active campaigner for human rights. Astrology is a big hit with many Aquarians, and you'll enjoy teaching yourself all about it. Group activities are another interest, and you're an avid member of all sorts of organizations and societies.

 **Pisces**

Anything artistic or creative is perfect for you, because you have abundant gifts at your disposal. Painting, drawing, writing poetry and dancing are all classic Piscean pastimes. In fact, you may feel rather fed up or stifled when you can't express yourself creatively. When you want to escape from the world, you love going to the cinema or the theatre. You're a Water sign so you enjoy any activities connected with water, such as swimming or other forms of water sports. Many Pisceans enjoy gardening, and you'll especially like having some form of water feature in your garden even if it's very modest. You're very musical, and would enjoy learning to play an instrument if you can't already do so. You might also like using your psychic talents, perhaps by learning to read the tarot or runes.

♈ Aries

Ariens love to keep active, so you aren't interested in any sort of hobby that's very sedentary or that keeps you glued to the sofa. You much prefer being kept busy, especially if it's out of doors. You also have a strong sense of adventure and a great love of speed, so one hobby that's right up your street is motor-racing. You might be lucky enough to be the driver, or you could be a spectator shouting yourself hoarse from the stands, but this is a sport you love. Speaking of sports, anything that's competitive and which threatens to knock the stuffing out of you will also suit you down to the ground. Rugby, football and baseball all fit the bill, and you might also enjoy martial arts and Eastern forms of exercise such as T'ai Chi.

THE YEAR 2000

 Friends and Lovers

There's a distinct flavour of romance in the air as the year begins. What a great start to 2000! However, you may not want to shout your feelings from the rooftops, and it's far more likely that you'll prefer to keep your emotions to yourself. That might be because they're very private and not for public consumption, or it could be because you're involved in a behind-the-scenes alliance that no one else must know about. Either way, there's a lot to enjoy during the first six weeks of 2000.

After that, you really come into your own. Starting from Valentine's Day, your confidence blossoms and you begin to stand out from the crowd. If you want to push yourself forward in some way, or you long to tell someone how you feel, this is the ideal opportunity to do so. You're riding high in the popularity stakes, too, so you may meet some new friends or be in great demand socially. You'll certainly be kept busy!

You're in quite a self-sufficient mood in the first eight months of the year, and you'll enjoy your own company.

Of course, that doesn't mean you won't like being sociable, but you'll certainly benefit from having some time to yourself every now and then. You may also find that other people rely on you a lot, perhaps because they think you're very strong and dependable at the moment. That's great, but don't let anyone take advantage of you.

Over the past couple of years there have been times when it's been hard to work out what older friends and relatives expect from you, and this feeling will continue in 2000. Make sure that you're honest and straightforward whenever possible, so you have no reason to reproach yourself if confusion arises.

Health

Good news! With Jupiter, the planet of good fortune, speeding through your sign this year, you're bound to feel full of beans. That's especially likely between February and June, when you'll be a walking advert for good health and you'll have an abundance of energy. If you've been feeling under the weather recently, all that will change when you start to perk up again. You might even hear some great news if you've been waiting for the results of a hospital test or investigation.

Unfortunately, you might also put on some extra weight that you don't want. That's because your willpower could go by the board when you succumb to lots of edible temptations. Favourite foods, delectable treats, delicious drinks – they could all go down the hatch and end up decorating your waistline or hips. Not that you'll mind at the time because you'll really be enjoying yourself, but you could regret all that feasting when you discover that your clothes have shrunk in the wardrobe. So, if you already battle with your weight, try to exercise a little moderation in the food and drink stakes during the first half of the year.

This is certainly an excellent year to concentrate on improving your health and fitness. Think about what you can do to get yourself in the peak of condition, but make sure you don't overdo it. Choose forms of exercise that make you gently puffed, as opposed to leaving you panting on the floor waiting for the room to stop whirling around. You might even start a health regime that you'll be able to continue for months, or perhaps years, to come.

 **Money**

Hooray! It promises to be one of those enjoyable years when you're in the money. However, unless you keep fairly tight control over your spending habits, you could end 2000 having spent as much as you gained. You might even find that you've spent more than you've received! Money will burn a big hole in your pocket, especially when it comes to buying items that belong to the fun-filled categories of treats, luxuries and indulgences. You won't be able to stop yourself!

Ideally, you should set aside some money for enjoyment and salt away the rest in a savings scheme or some other provision for a firm financial future. That may not sound very exciting but it is certainly prudent, and in a few years' time you could have good reason to thank your lucky stars that you did this. Nevertheless, this is a great year for spending your money on items that will bring you pleasure and which will grow in value over the years. So you might invest some money in an antique, or you could put your hard-earned cash into bricks and mortar. Beware of get-rich-quick schemes, because they could easily leave you with egg on your face, or they might fail to live up to expectations.

If you share your resources with another person, perhaps through a joint account, you may have to do some sorting out in 2000. This is especially likely if your birthday falls between 1 and 5 May, when you could be confronted by major changes to your finances. You may have to make new arrangements or you might have to bail out your partner when they come adrift financially. Whenever your birthday falls, 2000 is not a good year for trying to pull a fast one on the taxman or any other official financial organization. Be honest, otherwise you could be caught out!

 **Career**

Confidence is your middle name in 2000, helping you to stand out from the crowd. It's a marvellous year to channel your energies into new ventures and fresh initiatives, and the more exciting these are the more you'll want them to succeed. You could become rather fed up with anything old hat or which has outlived its usefulness, and the events that take place around the Eclipsed Full Moon on 21 January will leave you feeling unsettled and eager for new horizons. You may also have to find a balance between the demands of work and those of your home life.

So try to set your sights on new ideas whenever you get the chance. That doesn't mean abandoning your current job or career simply for the sake of it, but it does involve adopting a fresh approach if you suspect you're getting rather bogged down. Don't be frightened to take the initiative or to strike out in new directions. You might get the chance to work from home if you've worked in an office until now, or you might realize that it's the right opportunity to become freelance or to set up your own business.

There will be times when it's difficult to keep a boss or superior happy. They may keep changing their mind about what they want from you, or they could blow hot and cold so that you feel confused. The best way to handle this is to stick to your guns and make sure that you're doing your best. You should also avoid telling any little white lies when the going gets tough. Honesty is your best policy in 2000!

Your Day by Day Guide

JANUARY AT A GLANCE

Love	♥ ♥ ♥
Money	£ $ £
Career	💻 💻 💻 💻 💻
Health	☼

• *Saturday 1 January* •

It's a wonderful start to the new millennium because you're feeling tremendously positive and optimistic. The next few days will be a great opportunity to think about what you want to achieve in the coming year, and you'll be able to make plans that combine common sense with foresight and a sense of adventure. You're particularly interested in activities that will teach you more about the world.

• *Sunday 2 January* •

Today is a lovely, gentle day, so try to put your feet up at some point or cuddle up with a very special person. You're able to give someone the benefit of the doubt today, and you'll automatically assume the best rather than the worst. If you're working, you'll have a good chance to have a quiet word in someone's ear, especially if you want them to do you a favour or you need the benefit of their advice.

• *Monday 3 January* •

You're in a delightfully loving and affectionate mood today, so it's the perfect opportunity to get together with someone who occupies a very special place in your heart. Let them know how you feel, or buy them a little gift if you want to be generous. You're also feeling very ardent now, so you might decide that actions speak louder than words. Watch out for someone who seems to be slightly jealous or possessive.

• Tuesday 4 January •

Channel your energies into your future plans and wishes over the coming month. Think hard about what you want to do this year, and then start to map out your strategy. This is also a marvellous time to concentrate on your social life and your friendships. How about joining a club or society if you want to meet some new people? A hobby or pastime will also be exciting and enjoyable now.

• Wednesday 5 January •

If you're involved in a discussion or debate today you'll find it easy to speak up and say what you think. What's more, other people will listen to you! If you want to encourage a friend to do something, this is the day to chivvy them along. It's also a good opportunity to plan an outing or weekend break so you've got something to look forward to, especially if you're feeling a bit flat after the festivities.

• Thursday 6 January •

Your powers of concentration are ace today, making it an ideal time to study a subject in depth or apply your considerable brainpower to a knotty question. Listen carefully to what someone tells you now, because it will provide you with plenty of food for thought and it could also contain an important lesson. A philosophical, religious or environmental subject will teach you a lot about the world.

• Friday 7 January •

The more open-minded and optimistic you can be during the coming fortnight, the more you'll benefit. It's definitely not a time for standing on the sidelines wondering whether you should do something. Instead, you need to throw yourself wholeheartedly into activities and explore new horizons. Maybe you fancy doing some travelling or perhaps you'd prefer some armchair travel in the shape of a correspondence course or an interesting book? Whatever appeals, start doing it now.

• *Saturday 8 January* •

Get set for a difficult day, when a certain person is about as much fun as a wet blanket. They may pour cold water on all your ideas or they could be full of doom and gloom so that you quickly catch their miserable mood. Work or other responsibilities could interfere with today's plans, which will make you feel restricted and hampered. Try to introduce some light relief. You'll need it!

• *Sunday 9 January* •

A certain person is caught in the grip of some very powerful and intense emotions today. That's wonderful if you share these feelings, because you'll both be in an emotional world of your own. But the trouble will start if one of you wants to have a moody and dramatic encounter while the other one has very different ideas. Try to control any hints of jealousy, especially if you're the one who's feeling this way.

• *Monday 10 January* •

Today's mood is much lighter than in recent days, thank goodness, which gives you a breather if you were starting to feel bogged down. You'll make a lot of progress in your career or in a relationship with an authority figure now if you can introduce some humour. Get them laughing or show that you don't have to take life seriously to be a success. It's a good day to ask someone a favour, especially if they can pull strings on your behalf.

• *Tuesday 11 January* •

A chum is a true friend today, bending over backwards to help you or to be around when you need them. They could do you a good turn or give you some excellent advice. Alternatively, you'll perform this service for them, in which case you'll be pleased to do whatever you can to help. It's also a good day for taking concrete action that will bring a future plan one step nearer to reality.

• *Wednesday 12 January* •

If personal plans haven't been going the way you'd like recently, thank goodness they start to return to normal from now. It's an excellent day for making decisions, provided you're absolutely sure that you won't change your mind at a later date and that you're happy with what you've opted to do. It's also a terrific opportunity to launch a new project, especially if it has serious overtones.

• *Thursday 13 January* •

Your emotions take an intense turn today, so that you take life a lot more seriously than usual. It's a wonderful opportunity to draw closer to a certain someone, especially if you're both honest about your feelings and your hopes for your shared future. It's also a good chance to make some changes to your relationship, whether they're major or minor.

• *Friday 14 January* •

Travel plans could be interrupted or even stymied today, so take care if you're out and about. You may not hear some vital information until it's too late to do anything about it. Watch out for someone who gets on their high horse or who lectures you about something, even though you're not interested in what they've got to say. You could also be offended by some-one's thoughtless remark.

• Saturday 15 January •

Try to pace yourself today because you don't have as much energy as usual. Make sure that you take plenty of breaks if you're doing something strenuous, and keep well away from people who are germ factories in case they're generous enough to pass some bugs on to you. However, it's a good day for working hard on a personal plan, especially if you can concentrate on it to the exclusion of all else.

• Sunday 16 January •

Grab any opportunity to broaden your horizons today, whether you do it mentally, physically or spiritually. You'll enjoy curling up with a good book or watching a fascinating TV programme, or you might have an interesting conversation with someone. If you need to study for an exam or test, you'll make a lot of progress now. Even so, make sure you have a break at some point, otherwise you'll run out of steam.

• Monday 17 January •

It's another day when you'll benefit from concentrating on your plans and wishes for the future. You're filled with enthusiasm and the determination to get ahead, yet you're also able to make good decisions about what's feasible and what isn't. It's a good move to share your plans with a friend or associate and sound them out, because they could have some great insights or ideas.

• Tuesday 18 January •

Think carefully about your career and public reputation over the next couple of weeks. Talk to people who can point you in the right direction, whether they're friends or professional advisers. Meetings, appointments and discussions will also go well now because you've got the confidence to say what you think and you've also got the leadership qualities needed to make people sit up and take notice of you. It's an excellent time to apply for a new job.

• *Wednesday 19 January* •

Take care today because a certain someone is being very wilful and headstrong. They won't be keen to negotiate if you don't agree with them, and they may even talk your ears off in their attempts to persuade you round to their point of view. Watch out, too, for any hint of jealousy or possessiveness. Trying to restrict someone's freedom or acting as if you own them will provoke a huge backlash, so be careful!

• *Thursday 20 January* •

If you've been slogging away recently and feel you haven't received any recognition for your efforts, all that might be about to change. Over the next four weeks you could finally receive a few pats on the back – or better! It's also a terrific time to talk to a boss about promotion, to look for a more rewarding job or to put yourself up for election or anything else that will put you in the public eye. Good luck!

• *Friday 21 January* •

Today's Full Moon throws the spotlight on your family life, and will continue to do so for the next two weeks. You may have to sort out a tricky problem, especially if you've got to tread a fine line between the demands of your work and those of your nearest and dearest. Don't expect the answer to be a simple one. You may have to weigh up the pros and cons and settle for a compromise.

• *Saturday 22 January* •

What a lovely day! You're all set to enjoy yourself, so try to throw yourself into the social round whenever you get the chance. Get together with a special person or round up some chums and go out for a meal together. It's also a fabulous day for going shopping with your other half, and you could snap up a few bargains connected with a favourite hobby. Love or affection will blossom between you and a friend.

• Sunday 23 January •

Try to set aside some time today when you can be by yourself. It will be very valuable to think carefully about your love life or your relationship with a certain someone, especially if you're looking for ways to improve things. This is a great day for putting a liaison on a more solid footing, perhaps by making some form of emotional commitment to this person or by telling them how you feel.

• Monday 24 January •

Your sign of Taurus may not be noted for its love of adventure, but you get the chance to rise to challenges over the next four weeks and you'll love every minute of it! So be prepared to branch out in new directions. If you're thinking about booking up this year's holiday, how about visiting somewhere you've never been before? You could fall for someone from a different culture or walk of life now, or you might lose your heart to a campaign or a particular interest.

• Tuesday 25 January •

There's a rather subdued atmosphere today and you're reluctant to stick your neck out too far. It's difficult to communicate with an authority figure because they're being po-faced, critical or disapproving – or are you simply afraid of incurring their displeasure? It's one of those days when it's hard to know whether the problems are caused by a lack of confidence on your part or the stern attitude of other people. Maybe it's six of one and half a dozen of the other?

• *Wednesday 26 January* •

If you've been trying to sort out a financial problem, or you haven't made much progress recently with a bureaucratic tangle, roll up your sleeves today. You'll make a lot of headway, especially if you're single-minded and you don't take your eye off the ball. You'll also be able to unravel any mysteries that have been puzzling you recently, so you can get to the bottom of what's going on.

• *Thursday 27 January* •

You're in a terrific mood today – good-humoured, generous and light-hearted. Unfortunately, work doesn't come very high on your list of priorities so it will be a struggle to keep your nose to the grindstone. If you're following a diet or trying to give up a bad health habit, it may be almost impossible to summon up the required willpower today. Maybe you should indulge yourself a little and then return to the straight and narrow?

• *Friday 28 January* •

Tread carefully if you're involved in an official or bureaucratic agreement or discussion today, because certain people are a law unto themselves. You can't count on them, because they could change their minds or adopt a completely different attitude from the one you were expecting. If you're concentrating on something that's as dry as dust, try to vary it with tasks that are more interesting, otherwise you'll end up at screaming pitch.

• *Saturday 29 January* •

It seems that you can't do a thing right today. Or so a certain someone keeps telling you. They may tick you off about something that you consider to be trivial, or you may get the distinct impression that you're falling far short of their high standards. Are you being sloppy or are they being a real nit-picker? If you've been promising yourself not to mention a certain subject, you could blurt it out now in a fit of pique. What a day!

• Sunday 30 January •

Enjoy the company of people who are older or wiser than you today. Have a chat with them, especially if they want to wander down memory lane or they have a fascinating story to tell you. Take care if you're sorting out a financial or official matter because someone may not give you the correct information or you could overlook an important point. Ideally, it's a day for relaxing rather than working.

• Monday 31 January •

Take care because there's a tense atmosphere at work. You may feel that you let yourself down or you could be confronted by the results of some previous actions that you hoped everyone had forgotten about. Not so, it seems. There could also be an unpleasant run-in with someone who's dictatorial, unbending or a stickler for details. Have some light relief at some point, otherwise you'll soon feel exhausted.

FEBRUARY AT A GLANCE

Love	♥ ♥ ♥
Money	£
Career	💻 💻 💻 💻 💻
Health	☼ ☼ ☼ ☼

• Tuesday 1 February •

If you've been trying to sort out a financial or official matter that's had you going round in circles, you'll get another chance today to play detective and find out what's happening.

It's also an excellent opportunity to have a serious talk with someone, especially if you want to thrash out the difficulties between you and find a solution that you're both happy with.

• *Wednesday 2 February* •

If you're still thinking about where to go on holiday this year, this is a great day for visiting your travel agent and coming home with an armful of brochures. It's a wonderful day for drawing closer to someone by having an in-depth talk with them, particularly if you're prepared to open up and discuss some far-ranging subjects. Adopting an optimistic approach to life has some great rewards now.

• *Thursday 3 February* •

Channel all your efforts into your hopes and dreams for the future today. The more positive you are about these, the better their chance of coming to fruition. However, make sure that you're not simply indulging in wishful thinking, because that won't get you very far at all. A friend's enthusiasm for a hobby or activity will bowl you over so that you get equally excited about it.

• *Friday 4 February* •

It's a great day for taking part in a business meeting, important discussion or job interview because you're feeling so open-minded and positive. You'll be able to show that you're a valuable member of any team, and you could also give someone some excellent advice. If you have expert knowledge about something, this could be your chance to dazzle people with your abilities.

• *Saturday 5 February* •

Now that you've had time to think about what you want to achieve in your career or with your long-term goals, you can start putting those ideas into action. Concentrate over the coming fortnight on ways in which you can advertise your talents or put your name in lights. You don't have to do everything at once, but don't miss this chance to get the ball rolling and create your own future.

• *Sunday 6 February* •

Take care today that things might not always go according to plan. This could be really annoying for you, especially if you're interrupted by all sorts of unforeseen or irritating incidents. Someone you were counting on could let you down or you may face enormous resistance when you suggest making some changes. An authority figure will be very hard to handle.

• *Monday 7 February* •

What have you got planned this week? If there's nothing to look forward to, try to change that by making some social arrangements or organizing an outing with a friend. It's a lovely day for concentrating on a hobby or pastime, especially if you want a break from your usual routine. You could also hear some very useful information about something that you're planning for the future.

• *Tuesday 8 February* •

Keep a tight grip on your temper if you're out with friends today, otherwise you could blurt out something that's better left unsaid. Or is it? You're certainly feeling rather hot under the collar now, but you may think that it's better to pretend nothing's wrong rather than to let someone know that they're annoying you. However, matters could be taken out of your hands when you reach the end of your tether and say exactly what you're thinking. Whoops!

• *Wednesday 9 February* •

It's a day for taking life gently whenever you get the chance. If you're busy at work it could be hard to get down to it in the way you'd like. Your mind may keep drifting off to other subjects, or you could become engrossed in an interesting conversation with a colleague. Listen to your hunches now, because they could be a lot more accurate than you imagine.

• *Thursday 10 February* •

Today is great for winning someone's co-operation or assistance, simply through the sheer force of your personality. So you've got good reason to feel confident if you're off to a job interview, career assessment or important meeting. You'll also achieve a lot if you spend time having a serious conversation with someone whose opinions you respect. You might even find yourself confiding in this person.

• *Friday 11 February* •

It's very difficult to understand what a certain person wants today. They may say one thing and then do another, or it may be almost impossible to get a straight answer out of them. Watch out if this is a boss or authority figure, because they may imagine that they've given you clear instructions, even though you don't have a clue what they're on about. A charity or good cause wins your support.

• *Saturday 12 February* •

Your energy levels take a slight nose-dive from today, and they won't be back on form until late March. In the meantime there will be occasions when you find it difficult to stand up for yourself. You may also have problems asking for what you want, perhaps because you think you don't deserve it or because you don't know how to find the right words. Try to be aware of this, otherwise it could make you frustrated.

• *Sunday 13 February* •

Someone seems to have a bee in their bonnet today, and you won't be able to budge it. They could end up sounding like a broken record as they endlessly drone on, or maybe you're the one whose conversational needle has got stuck? You may object to the way a certain person is behaving, but be warned that trying to restrict their freedom is the best way to lose them right now.

• *Monday 14 February* •

It's Valentine's Day and, sure enough, you've got a lot to smile about, whether or not the post has brought you a card. Jupiter, the planet of good fortune, moves into your own sign today, heralding an enjoyable time when your self-confidence rises, opportunities come your way and you feel expansive, good-tempered and gregarious. If life is what you make it, you've got the chance of cooking up something wonderful now.

• *Tuesday 15 February* •

Focus on your finances today, especially if you need to pay some bills or sort out a slight difficulty. It's also a great day to consult someone and ask their expert opinion. Any activities connected with your career or public standing will go well, and if you're in the limelight today you'll really enjoy yourself. It's also a good day for making an important or major investment.

• *Wednesday 16 February* •

You excel in conversations, meetings and discussions today. That's because you're able to speak up and say what you think, but you're also blessed with a huge helping of common sense and practicality. This combination means that people will sit up and take notice whenever you open your mouth. If you've been procrastinating about writing a tricky letter or making an awkward phone call, take a deep breath and do it today.

• *Thursday 17 February* •

It's easy to get het up about someone or something today, especially if it has a spiritual, religious or political connection. This is a good opportunity to let off some steam, particularly if you've been holding in your feelings recently, but don't let things get out of hand or take the whole thing too seriously. Watch out for a woman who's manipulative or competing for someone's attention.

• *Friday 18 February* •

You'll really enjoy making progress in your career during the next three weeks, and you could also get a lot of help in the guise of a certain someone. This person may take you under their wing or give you lots of useful advice. You could be attracted to someone now who has a lot more power, money or status than you. Be honest with yourself about why this person has such an effect on you. Is it because of *what* they are rather than *who* they are?

• *Saturday 19 February* •

Today's Full Moon is urging you to bring a current difficulty or problem with a loved one to a gentle close over the next two weeks. This may involve having a few words with them, or maybe you can be a little more subtle than that? You may also have to admit that something you were looking forward to isn't going to happen in the way you had hoped, or maybe it has to be cancelled altogether. *C'est la vie.*

• *Sunday 20 February* •

A friend is a real live wire today, and tremendous fun to have around. In fact, you'll really feel that you're missing out if you can't spend time with other people now. Arrange a get-to-gether at the last minute or decide to visit a mate on the spur of the moment. You'll also enjoy working on a pastime or hobby, especially if it lets you forget about any current worries or problems.

• *Monday 21 February* •

Mind how you go in all future plans between now and the middle of March because things won't always run as smoothly as you'd like. Someone could get hold of the wrong end of the stick or you may find it difficult to get in touch with the very person you need to contact. It may not be easy to get hold of friends, either – someone may always be out or their phone could go on the blink.

• *Tuesday 22 February* •

Take care today because it's awfully easy to put someone on a lofty pedestal and then feel deeply disappointed when they reveal that they're only human after all. So beware of idealizing someone or, for that matter, expecting far too much from yourself. It's not advisable to sign on any dotted lines today unless you're 100 per cent sure of what you're doing.

• *Wednesday 23 February* •

Try to vary your routine as much as possible today, especially if you're at work. You'll find it much easier to settle down to the chores if you can have frequent breaks, and you'll prefer to work on new projects whenever possible. A colleague or client has some interesting news, and you'll like their refreshing viewpoint of the world. It's a great day for being inventive.

• *Thursday 24 February* •

The more sociable you are today, the better you'll like it. So try not to spend too much time alone if you can possibly avoid it. If you don't have anything planned for the weekend ahead, start getting on the phone and making some arrangements. It's a great day for discussing a problem with someone because you could come up with a solution. Two heads are definitely better than one now.

• Friday 25 February •

Yesterday you felt very sociable. Today, you'll probably prefer to be left to your own devices. That's because other people are so hard to get along with. They may be remote, off-hand or unfriendly, or you may get the impression that they're looking down their noses at you. Is that true or are you simply being over-sensitive? Try not to imagine that things are worse than they really are.

• Saturday 26 February •

It would be a good idea to take life easy whenever you get the chance today. If you're not working, then put your feet up and leave the chores alone. You know they'll still be there when you're ready for them! It's a lovely day for enjoying the company of a close partner or an older friend, even if neither of you does anything very energetic or special. Simply relaxing in front of the TV or watching a video will do very nicely.

• Sunday 27 February •

Happily it's easy to get on well with other people today because you're keen to live and let live. So if you often avoid seeing an older relative, because they can drive you demented, this is a good day to get in touch – your tolerance levels are so much higher than usual. If you're working, you could be strongly attracted to someone you meet, especially if some sort of mystery surrounds them.

• Monday 28 February •

If you've been sailing a bit too close to the financial wind recently, you could receive a nasty ticking off from your bank manager today. Alternatively, you may realize that you've got to do some economizing or that something costs a lot more than you'd expected. It's not a good day to apply for a loan or ask someone a financial favour because the answer is likely to be 'no'. A boss isn't exactly a barrel of laughs. What a day!

• Tuesday 29 February •

It's horribly easy to get hold of the wrong end of the stick today, and then to worry about what you think you've discovered. So try to take with a pinch of salt any suspicions or worries that dawn on you now. For instance, you might see evidence that convinces you someone is being unfaithful, even though they're perfectly innocent. It will be hard to make contact with a friend or lover.

MARCH AT A GLANCE

Love	♥ ♥ ♥
Money	£
Career	💻 💻 💻 💻
Health	☼ ☼ ☼

• Wednesday 1 March •

Someone's very chatty today. So chatty, in fact, that before too long you could get rather fed up with hearing the sound of their voice. However, they may not notice this because they'll be so busy telling you everything in minute detail. You could also hear some gossip, but be careful about who you pass it on to in case you let any cats out of bags. Even so, it's a great day for social events.

• Thursday 2 March •

Concentrate on your future plans and wishes today. Think seriously about what you want to achieve and how you're going to go about it. It's also a good idea to pick the brains of someone who can give you a few hints or even provide you with some valuable contacts. A friend is great company now, sensible, practical and matter of fact. Indeed, you'll be very pleased with everything that happens today.

• *Friday 3 March* •

You may be fed up with the direction in which a friendship or close relationship is heading, and become eager to make some significant changes. Today, however, you'll get nowhere fast, because it seems that someone is very resistant to your ideas. They may feel threatened by them or they may object to your thoughts on principle, and that won't please you one bit. Beware of becoming equally stubborn just to spite them. Where will that get you?

• *Saturday 4 March* •

Mind how you go when dealing with a boss or someone in power today because they could behave in ways that you don't expect. You certainly shouldn't underestimate them or imagine that you can steal a march on them, because you'll soon find otherwise. There's a chance that you could fall for someone today, in which case they may be very different from your usual type.

• *Sunday 5 March* •

Friends make your world go round today, so try to get together with some chums at some point. You don't have to do anything very special together – simply sharing a meal or going for a drink will be good fun. A hobby or pastime will give you a much-needed break from the demands of work, especially if you're still recovering from what happened yesterday.

• *Monday 6 March* •

Today's New Moon is urging you to turn over a new leaf in your plans and wishes for the future. This area of your life has been highlighted over the past few weeks, and now's your chance to think about all that you've learned and to put your ideas into action. Get cracking over the coming fortnight, while the New Moon is able to add force to your decisions and give them the best possible start.

• *Tuesday 7 March* •

You have a strong urge to be your own boss today, especially if you're expected to knuckle under and follow someone else's orders. You might even think about changing jobs so you've got more scope to do your own thing, or perhaps you've been flirting with the idea of becoming self-employed and it's now becoming an even more attractive option than before? If possible, discuss your thoughts with someone whose opinions you respect.

• *Wednesday 8 March* •

There's a strong emotional link between you and a certain someone today, and it will give you a warm sense of satisfaction and comfort. In fact, you could become so close to one another that your relationship is transformed in some way. Perhaps you're more able to trust one another or you'll see a private side of each other that you've never glimpsed before?

• *Thursday 9 March* •

It's a day for making plans, although you may not be able to put them into practice straightaway. Even so, that shouldn't stop you from thinking about what you want to achieve in the next few months. If an invitation comes along today you'll want to grab it, because you're in a delightfully sociable mood.

You'll also benefit from talking to someone from another country or walk of life.

• *Friday 10 March* •

If you've been at cross-purposes with a friend recently or something went wrong between you, this is a great opportunity to discuss what happened and then put the whole thing behind you. You're in a very outgoing mood today, so try not to spend too much time by yourself. You could become involved in an altruistic or high-minded campaign or activity.

• *Saturday 11 March* •

Today you're in a great mood, determined to enjoy yourself whenever you get the chance. And that's where the trouble will start, because the one thing you're not keen on now is discipline. So if there's something you're supposed to do, it may take a lot of effort to make yourself get round to it. You'll find all sorts of excuses to postpone it, but it would be far better to get it out of the way so you don't have to think about it any longer.

• *Sunday 12 March* •

You're in a very easy-going frame of mind today and will do your best to get on well with whoever happens to be around. Someone may use you as a confidante, especially if they've been going through a hard time recently or they're in need of someone who can listen without being judgemental. Use your imagination if you're working, and try to concentrate on creative activities rather than hard facts.

• *Monday 13 March* •

You've been working very hard recently but from today you get a little light relief in the shape of an enhanced social life. Expect to receive lots of invitations over the next three weeks, and you might also issue a few of your own. It's a wonderful time to increase your circle of friends, especially if you fancy joining a club or organization that caters for people who share some of your own interests.

• Tuesday 14 March •

There's been a tricky communications gap between you and certain people recently but things start to get back on an even keel now. So if you've been worried about repairing your relationship, start making amends today. This is an excellent day to make a serious decision about your hopes and wishes for the future, especially if you've realized what your next step should be. Now's the time to take it.

• Wednesday 15 March •

It's definitely a day for being sociable and gregarious, and you'll feel really left out if you have to spend too long by yourself. It's a terrific day for going on a date with someone, whether you know them almost as well as you know yourself or you've only just met. Either way, you're a very charming companion and they'll thoroughly enjoy your company.

• Thursday 16 March •

Tread carefully now because things may not be quite what they seem. Someone may make you promises that they have no intention of keeping, or they could tell you things that are true at the time but which soon change. Beware of a tendency to imagine that someone is almost superhuman or to expect great things of them when you know from experience that they won't deliver the goods.

• Friday 17 March •

Because it's a very restless day, you'll find it hard to settle to anything for long. For a start, that's because you're feeling agitated and edgy, and this won't be helped by lots of silly interruptions or annoying distractions. If you're working at home today, be prepared for all sorts of irritations to get in the way or interfere with your concentration. Try to work on something interesting or unusual.

• Saturday 18 March •

It's a lovely day for going shopping, because you're really in the mood to enjoy yourself. You could be drawn to shops that cater for one of your interests, and you'll also get a kick out of meeting friends for a drink or a meal. You'll benefit from someone's generosity of spirit, even if they can't afford to be generous with their cash. All in all, it's a really great day, so have fun!

• Sunday 19 March •

Try to spend today with people that you care about. You don't have to do anything very special together, you'll simply appreciate their company. However, you may also benefit from having a little time to yourself, especially if you can do something creative or artistic at the same time. If there's an emotional crisis today you'll be able to cope wonderfully well, so expect people to rely on you.

• Monday 20 March •

Today's Full Moon is reminding you that you need to finish off any projects you're currently engaged in that allow you to express some of your many talents. You may also have to iron out an emotional difficulty with someone, especially if it's been dragging on for some time. Be prepared to accept that the past is over and that it's time to set your sights on the future instead.

• Tuesday 21 March •

It's a great day for making progress at work or in a joint financial matter. You'll be able to get people on your side and you'll also find it easy to explain how you'd like them to help you. If you've been finding it difficult to get on well with someone, this is a good opportunity to talk things through and find a solution that suits both of you.

• *Wednesday 22 March* •

Take care if you're at work today because it will be hard to fathom what a boss or partner is talking about. They may be sending out mixed messages, or you could feel that they're barking up the wrong tree. There's also the potential for a lot of confusion if you're attending a meeting or appointment, so double-check anything that you don't understand.

• *Thursday 23 March* •

Your energy levels start to rise today, and they'll continue to climb until early May. During this time you'll feel able to stand up for yourself if necessary, and you'll also be blessed with a lot more confidence than usual. That's ideal if you need the impetus and enthusiasm to launch a new project or get something off the ground. However, watch out for a tendency to be argumentative when you don't get your own way!

• *Friday 24 March* •

Partnerships leave a lot to be desired today. That's because things will go wrong between you. If you've arranged to meet someone, you might spend a long time hanging around because you've both got different times in your diaries. Or you could fall out with someone over a silly little spat that wouldn't normally bother you at all. Try not to enter into a partnership with someone if you can avoid it now.

• *Saturday 25 March* •

A friend is a tremendous help to you today. They may simply be there when you need them or they could give you some great advice. It's a lovely day for going out with a chum, especially if you're visiting somewhere beautiful or relaxing. You'll also enjoy working on a favourite hobby. Group activities will go well and you'll have an interesting encounter with someone.

● *Sunday 26 March* ●

You're in a very compassionate and sympathetic frame of mind today, and if someone needs a shoulder to cry on you'll do your best to help. So be prepared to listen to a tale of woe or to give some advice. If you're currently involved in a charitable activity, it could keep you pretty busy because you may have to take over someone else's responsibilities or a certain person may appeal to your better nature and ask you to lend a hand.

● *Monday 27 March* ●

You're in a nicely adventurous mood today and will happily rise to whichever challenges life places in your path. It's a great day for arranging a short break or a long weekend, especially if you're starting to get itchy feet and you fancy a change of scene. You could also be interested in some form of further education, whether it's very ambitious or it's something quite simple. You're in the mood to learn more about the world.

● *Tuesday 28 March* ●

If you've been biting your tongue recently and promising yourself that you wouldn't say anything about the irritating behaviour or rude attitude of a certain person, think again! This looks like being the day when your feelings flood out in a great rush. You may feel guilty about it at the time but once you've calmed down you'll be relieved that everything is finally out in the open.

• *Wednesday 29 March* •

Be careful if you're doing anything connected with travel today, because things won't always go as smoothly as you expect. If you're catching a train or a bus it could be delayed or even cancelled, or there could be a hold-up if you're driving. It's not a good day to make any holiday arrangements because there's too much scope for things to go wrong. It's the same story if you want to organize some further education.

• *Thursday 30 March* •

Someone or something has been bothering you quite a bit recently, but today you get the chance finally to do something about it. Rather than worrying endlessly or having the whole thing go round and round in your head, it will be far more productive to take the bull by the horns now and do some-thing positive. This is also an excellent day to sort out a financial problem before it gets any worse.

• *Friday 31 March* •

Be choosy about who you trust today. Someone may promise to do something and then let you down, or you may be the one who's full of good intentions that fail to see the light of day. Watch your back if you've fallen out recently with some-one who has a high opinion of themselves, because they could try to seek their revenge now and it won't be in ways you were expecting. They'll be sneaky or malicious, or they could do something underhand. Take care!

APRIL AT A GLANCE

Love	♥ ♥ ♥ ♥
Money	£
Career	💻 💻
Health	☼ ☼

• *Saturday 1 April* •

It's a day for being sociable, especially if you can get together with some of your favourite chums. Try to do something lively or energetic together – you won't have much fun if you're stuck in one place for too long. It's also a great opportunity to get on with a pet hobby or pastime, particularly if it gets you out into the fresh air or introduces you to some like-minded people.

• *Sunday 2 April* •

Someone makes a very strong impression on you today, particularly if you already have an emotional connection with them. You'll get the chance really to appreciate being with this person, especially if you can have a serious talk about subjects that are important to you both. If you need to discuss something that is normally considered taboo or private, now's the time to speak up.

• *Monday 3 April* •

A woman will impress you greatly today. You may already know her, in which case she's probably a close friend, or you may meet her for the first time. If you're involved in a group activity, it will be easy to get on with the women there. What have you got planned for the week ahead? If your social life is sadly lacking, arrange something that you can look forward to.

• *Tuesday 4 April* •

Today's New Moon is urging you to turn over a new leaf in the most sensitive and private part of your life. Are there certain fears or worries that have been bugging you recently? Then spend part of the coming fortnight in facing up to them. You may even decide to take things one step further and consult an expert who can help you to surmount these obstacles and put them into their true perspective.

• *Wednesday 5 April* •

As a Taurean, you have a strong need for security in your life, and you're also resistant to change. But today finds you longing to break free in some way, even if it's only a very modest departure. Maybe you could make some changes to your work, or perhaps you could put a relationship with an authority figure on a new footing? You might also think up a new goal or ambition now that's very exciting.

• *Thursday 6 April* •

You're brimming with energy today, so put it to good use. Ideally, you should do something physical, such as going for a swim, taking a brisk walk, doing battle with the garden or traipsing off to the gym. If that isn't possible, maybe you could be active at home? Perhaps it's time to do some turning out or cleaning? However, don't take on more than you can manage, otherwise you'll start off in great style and then fizzle out halfway through.

• *Friday 7 April* •

It's almost impossible to second-guess a certain person today because they're a law unto themselves. They may say or do things that take you by complete surprise, especially if these are out of character or precisely what they said they *wouldn't* do. Watch out for someone in a position of power who's convinced that they're right and everyone else (and that includes you) is wrong.

• *Saturday 8 April* •

Going shopping today? Then you'll be drawn to items that are luxurious, sensuous or tactile. Unfortunately, they might also be quite expensive, but who's counting? Certainly not you, because it's one of those days when you'd rather forget about the state of your bank balance. However, if money really is thin on the ground you should be careful about spending it. Buy yourself a modest treat and then call it a day.

• *Sunday 9 April* •

What have you got planned for today? Anything that's very predictable or which smacks of routine will soon have you yawning faster than you can say 'I'm bored'. So try to break out of your usual Sunday schedule, especially if it involves spending time with people who are so predictable you could set your watch by them. You want to do something different for a change!

• *Monday 10 April* •

What's going on? Is there a strange atmosphere around a certain woman today? She may be feeling jealous or wary of you, but why? Maybe she feels that the two of you are competing with one another or perhaps you're simply caught in the firing line. These feelings may remain unspoken, so don't expect to be able to sort them out in one fell swoop. You may have to bide your time before you can ask what's wrong.

• *Tuesday 11 April* •

It's very easy, not to say tempting, to put someone on a lofty pedestal today. They may have already come pretty high in your pecking order, but today they're right up there at the top of your list of favourite people. That's wonderful, but try not to let your current admiration turn into something that's closely connected with idealism. If you do that, you could be in for a rude awakening later in the year.

• *Wednesday 12 April* •

What a wonderful day! You're in a fabulous mood – easy-going, gregarious and eager to get on well with everyone you encounter. Take care, however, if you're in the throes of a property deal or any other negotiations connected with your house, because it will be easy to get carried away or exaggerate something. If you're cooking, you'll probably make so much food that there are lots of lovely leftovers for tomorrow.

• *Thursday 13 April* •

Taureans are known as the strong and silent types, and from today you certainly come into that category. Between now and the end of the month there will be times when you'd rather keep quiet than speak up. However, be sensible about this and don't let your silence be misconstrued or used against you. You'd be wise to avoid any hint of gossip now, as it could backfire.

• *Friday 14 April* •

You're in a deliciously loving and affectionate mood today. It's a real pleasure for you to be with some of your favourite people, although you'll make a fuss of whoever is around you. Try to devote some time to a creative or artistic pursuit, because it will give you lots of emotional satisfaction. It's a lovely day for telling someone how much you care about them, so don't be shy!

• *Saturday 15 April* •

Mind how you go today because you could easily feel stymied or frustrated by the pattern of events. Things may be snarled up or delayed, or someone could pour cold water on a scheme that you thought was great. Try to channel this blocked energy into other activities so that you're able to salvage something from the day, otherwise you'll soon feel very fed up.

• *Sunday 16 April* •

It's difficult to understand what someone wants from you today. That might be because they're reluctant to say, or they expect you to guess. Or it might be because you secretly know exactly what they expect from you but you're not keen on giving it. It's easy to wear yourself out today, so try to take things gently. If you do get tired, you're likely to bite someone's head off.

• *Monday 17 April* •

An intense emotional bond links you to a certain person today and you'll really value it. It could be your passport to understanding this person's emotional state, and also what they expect from your relationship, so it could hold an invaluable lesson for you. Don't panic if you have an embarrassing or difficult encounter with someone. Try to extract the good things from your shared experience.

• *Tuesday 18 April* •

Today's Full Moon is reminding you that you need to start thinking about the state of your health. How are you feeling at the moment? Are you full of beans or do you drag yourself around sometimes? This is the perfect opportunity to sort out any health problems that are bothering you. The coming fortnight is also the time to get to grips with worries connected with your job or a colleague.

• *Wednesday 19 April* •

The Sun moves into your own sign today, making you feel a lot more energetic and confident than you've been in a while. You'll be in this happy state for the next four weeks, so use them well. How about launching a new venture or project, or maybe you'd prefer to concentrate on improving your personal life? This is when you can blossom and grow, so prepare to flourish!

• *Thursday 20 April* •

Oh dear, a certain person is a right old handful today. It seems that they're determined to be true to themselves, and apparently that means making everyone else's lives a misery. Be especially careful if this person happens to be a boss or authority figure, because it will be difficult for you to hide your irritation. If you're the one who wants to break free, try to do it in constructive and controlled ways. Don't create havoc just for the sake of it!

• *Friday 21 April* •

You're in a very contemplative and kind-hearted mood today. You may spend time with someone who's going through the mill at the moment, or you might look after an older friend or relative. If you need to unravel some red tape or sort out an official money matter, your best bet is to take things gently and treat everyone with diplomacy and consideration. This tactic will win people over.

• *Saturday 22 April* •

Intense emotions well up inside you today. Your initial instinct may be to repress them or ignore them, especially if they're connected with subjects that you'd rather not think about or which you consider to be off limits. But you'll find it's far easier, as well as being more productive, to accept the way that you're feeling. Watch out, however, for flashes of jealousy or revenge that rear their ugly heads.

• Sunday 23 April •

Try to give yourself a break from your usual routine today, otherwise you'll start to feel a bit agitated. It's especially important to have a breather if you're feeling overwhelmed by lots of responsibilities or demands from other people at the moment. Maybe you need to spend some time by yourself, doing something that's purely for you? An older friend or loved one has a surprise for you. Don't worry, it's a nice one!

• Monday 24 April •

What a wonderful day! You're in a terrific mood – open-minded, optimistic and eager to explore the world in any way you see fit. It's the perfect day to decide where you're going for your next holiday, or perhaps you'd prefer to book up a long weekend or short break. The idea of learning something new also appeals to you now, whether you do it in formal or informal ways.

• Tuesday 25 April •

It's another day when you need a break from your current responsibilities and obligations. Take yourself off for a couple of hours or, if possible, have a day's holiday from everything so you can return fresh tomorrow. You could hear something rather surprising during the course of the day, especially if it's also top secret or it's connected with someone in power.

• Wednesday 26 April •

Go carefully if you're at work or involved in a serious situation today, because there's enormous scope for mistakes and mis-understandings. Someone may give you some misleading information, or it might be almost impossible to get them motivated. Watch out, too, for someone who manages to sap your confidence or makes you feel demoralized. Are they justified in doing this?

• *Thursday 27 April* •

Prepare yourself for another day when people are hard to cope with. You might have to deal with someone in authority who tries to put you down or make you feel as if you can't do anything right. If you're attending an important meeting or interview, bolster your self-esteem by making sure you've got everything you need and, if necessary, reminding yourself of all your former triumphs.

• *Friday 28 April* •

A certain person is blessed with tremendous charm today, and don't you love it! They'll soon have you eating out of their hand, and you may find yourself confiding in them because they're so approachable. A romantic encounter could also be on the cards, when you-know-who sweeps you off your feet or whispers sweet nothings in your ear. You could also receive an affectionate letter or phone call.

• *Saturday 29 April* •

Spend today doing things that you enjoy with some of the people that you enjoy. A simple recipe for success! It's a day for being sociable and gregarious, so try not to spend too much time on your own. If you are left to your own devices, a pet hobby or pastime will fill you with satisfaction and completely engross you. You may also have a mind-expanding conversation with someone.

• *Sunday 30 April* •

You've felt quite tongue-tied over the past couple of weeks but from today you feel much more comfortable about speaking up. So grab every chance to boost your communications during the next two weeks. It's an excellent time for a serious discussion with someone, especially if you've got a lot of ground to cover or you need to talk about things that are very dear to your heart.

MAY AT A GLANCE

Love	❤ ❤ ❤ ❤ ❤
Money	£ $ £ $ £
Career	💻 💻 💻 💻 💻
Health	☼ ☼ ☼ ☼ ☼

• Monday 1 May •

Your charm rating starts to rise today, and it will stay in the ascendant until late May. So you can expect to attract many admirers now. In fact, this is a very powerful month for you, and by the time it ends you may feel very different from when it began. You might decide to alter your image in some way, or love could enter your life with such force that you're breathless.

• Tuesday 2 May •

It's difficult to settle down to your responsibilities and duties today. That may be because you'd rather be doing something more interesting and personally fulfilling, or it could be because events keep interrupting you. Go carefully if you're involved in big business or officialdom today because you might make some hasty decisions that you'll regret later on.

• Wednesday 3 May •

Proceed with extreme caution in all official dealings today because there's enormous scope for mistakes and slip-ups. If you've got to follow someone's instructions they may not make themselves properly understood, or they could change their mind after they've issued their orders. Be very wary about committing yourself to anything legal or binding today because you may not know what you're agreeing to. There could be dirty work afoot!

• Thursday 4 May •

Today's New Moon triggers a very important phase in your year. Over the coming fortnight you'll get the chance to branch out in exciting directions and embark on a new chapter in the story of your life. The changes and decisions that you take now will have enomous impact on you, so it's a fabulous time to take the plunge or embark on a new venture or association. You can achieve a tremendous amount now!

• Friday 5 May •

You benefit from someone's kindness and consideration today, especially if they're in a position of authority over you. You could discover that this person is a human being after all! You'll also get the chance to show some compassion to someone, perhaps when they ask your advice or bend your ear about some matter. It's a good day to buy something that's old or antique.

• Saturday 6 May •

If you put someone on a high pedestal last month, or thought that they were the best thing since chocolate pudding, the scales could tumble from your eyes today. You could be disappointed when this person lets you down or proves that they've got feet of clay after all. It's not a good idea to get involved in any agreements or negotiations today because someone may not be telling you the truth, even though they seem as nice as pie.

• Sunday 7 May •

Try to take things easy and relax today. You're not feeling very energetic and you'd much rather just coast along and take things as they come. It's easy to get on with women, and a female friend or relative is very helpful. You'll enjoy getting out into the fresh air, especially if you can visit some beautiful surroundings, such as a park, garden, the countryside or even an art gallery.

• Monday 8 May •

Enthusiasm and optimism radiate from every pore today, and you certainly know how to enjoy yourself. It's a fabulous day for making a big impression on other people, and if you need to muster your confidence you'll have no trouble in putting on a brave face. However, watch out for a tendency to take on too much or allow your positive approach to develop into a slight arrogance.

• Tuesday 9 May •

It's a wonderful day for concentrating on things that are important to you, especially if you need to do some serious thinking or talking about them. If you don't have anything engrossing to keep you occupied, your thoughts could turn rather gloomy or doom-laden. For instance, you might begin to worry about a personal issue or you could suffer from a lack of confidence.

• Wednesday 10 May •

You're capable of achieving a tremendous amount today, provided you roll your sleeves up. It's a marvellous day for concentrating on your priorities, and if you're worried about meeting a deadline you'll end up tired but happy with all that you've accomplished. You have a strong sense of responsibility now, which is great, but don't let anyone abuse it or take advantage of it.

• *Thursday 11 May* •

Yesterday you were blessed with ace powers of concentration. Today, it's difficult to settle down to anything for long. Maybe you keep being interrupted by trivia or perhaps you're simply not in the mood? You may also bridle at the obligations that are waiting for you. Watch out for a superior or boss who's acting so much out of character that you don't know where you stand.

• *Friday 12 May* •

It's a wonderfully sociable day so try to do something today, especially if you need to let off steam after the frustrating events of yesterday. Your love life is looking fabulous, so it's a great excuse to go out on the town with you-know-who. You don't need to spend a lot of money to have fun today, but you'll certainly adore splashing out on a few luxuries and treats.

• *Saturday 13 May* •

You're surrounded by a very strange atmosphere today. Events may be conspiring against you, so that even though you'd like to make progress in something you're being hampered or held back. Or maybe you're suddenly gripped by feelings of restlessness or rebellion that seem completely out of character. Alternatively, you'll meet these disruptive energies in someone else, so mind how you go with them.

• *Sunday 14 May* •

Think about your finances over the next couple of weeks, especially if you're aware that they need some attention. Write important letters or make some phone calls that will help to get matters sorted out. You might even decide to consult an expert, in which case this is the perfect time to ask for their advice. You should also spare a thought for your priorities in life. Do you devote enough time to them?

• *Monday 15 May* •

You can achieve a tremendous amount at work today, but things will go best if you can be inventive and original. This may go against the grain if you're the sort of Taurean who is anxious about stepping out of line, but this really is a great day to explore your creativity and express your individuality. If a health problem hasn't been helped by conventional medicine, consider an alternative treatment.

• *Tuesday 16 May* •

A certain person isn't making much sense today, and that will definitely cause problems if they happen to be your boss or partner. Should you try to follow their confused instructions or should you do what you think is best? Try to avoid getting involved in agreements or negotiations now because there's a major discrepancy between what someone says and what they mean.

• *Wednesday 17 May* •

Get set for one of the most enjoyable days of 2000. And if it's your birthday today, you can look forward to a fabulous year ahead! Try to get work or the chores out of the way as fast as possible, because you're in the mood to let your hair down and have fun. Your love life looks wonderful and your confidence soars. Someone could make your day, if not your month!

• *Thursday 18 May* •

You're in a much more sober mood than you were yesterday. In fact, you may even feel rather flat after yesterday's good humour. What's wrong? It's easy to read too much into situations today, especially if they have the potential to hurt you. You may suspect that someone is being tough on you or is giving you the cold shoulder, but is that really true? Maybe you're making mountains out of molehills?

• *Friday 19 May* •

A certain person digs their heels in today and refuses to budge. That's especially likely where finances are concerned, so if you were hoping to talk someone into seeing things from your point of view you'll be wasting your breath at the moment. Watch out for a whiff of jealousy or suspiciousness, when either you or your partner suspects that the other one is up to no good. What makes you so sure?

• *Saturday 20 May* •

Keep your options open today, otherwise you might miss a fabulous opportunity that comes along. It may boost your public reputation or social status, or it could be the lucky break you've been waiting for in your career. Alternatively, any feelings of restriction or limitation that have been nagging away at you recently really come to the fore today, making you long to jump ship and break free. But is that wise?

• *Sunday 21 May* •

Give yourself a break today by doing things that allow you to increase your mental and physical horizons. You might decide to visit a town or area that you've never seen before, or perhaps you'd prefer to curl up with a mind-expanding book. You're very receptive to other people's points of view now, so listen carefully to what they have to say. You could learn a lot.

• *Monday 22 May* •

It's another day when you long to explore new ideas and break fresh ground. Your usual routine simply isn't enough for you today. You need to get your teeth into something more challenging and adventurous. What do you fancy? Maybe you've been thinking about enrolling in an evening class or correspondence course, or perhaps you fancy reading a book on a subject that has always fascinated you. Something with global or international connections is important now.

• Tuesday 23 May •

Get to grips with your finances today, especially if that means seeking someone's expert advice or getting in touch with an official organization. Perhaps you need to fill in a complex form or make a few phone calls before you can get everything sorted out, but the results will be well worth the effort. It's also a great day for making plenty of progress on a project or long-term goal that means a lot to you.

• Wednesday 24 May •

Make the most of your good ideas today. Even though some may seem completely wacky or way off-centre, that doesn't mean you should dismiss them without further consideration. In fact, it's one of those days when original ideas and thoughts have a lot more potential than mundane notions. If you've been grappling with a long-standing problem, try approaching it from a fresh angle. Eureka!

• Thursday 25 May •

Money comes high up on your scale of priorities during the next couple of weeks. You're already in quite a fiscal state of mind but from today your cash begins to burn a hole in your pocket. You might be tempted to splash out on lots of treats and indulgences, whether or not you can afford them. But you'll also adore devoting yourself to the people and pastimes that make your world go round.

• Friday 26 May •

Take care today because certain people need to be treated with respect. Unfortunately, that may not be because you respect them but simply because they're likely to explode if you don't handle them with care. Watch out for a friend who's been bitten by the green-eyed monster and is envious of something you have, or a loved one who wants to tie you down. And try to avoid acting this way yourself.

• *Saturday 27 May* •

If you know that an older friend or relative has been going through the mill recently, get in touch with them today so they know you're thinking of them. They'll really appreciate it. If you're at work and it's often difficult to get on with your boss, make an effort to understand them today. It will be much easier than you imagine and you might even strike up an easy rapport.

• *Sunday 28 May* •

Should you be able to pull off a balancing act and combine optimism with common sense, you'll achieve a tremendous amount today. Think carefully about what you want to do over the next few months, then start planning your strategy. It's a very auspicious day for taking the initiative or embarking on a new venture, provided you've thought things through and you know exactly what you're doing.

• *Monday 29 May* •

It's a delightfully easy-going day and you want to take things gently. It's certainly not a day for racing around like a mad thing if you can possibly avoid it, because you may not have the stamina. Instead, you want to laze the day away or spend it with some very special people. If you're involved in a good cause it will go very well, or perhaps you'll decide that charity begins at home.

• *Tuesday 30 May* •

As far as you're concerned, a certain person can do no wrong today. You really respect and admire them, and you're honoured to know them. That's wonderful, but make sure your admiration doesn't turn into idealization or rose-tinted specs. Be careful, too, if you're involved in an important financial transaction, because you will be easily swayed by other people's arguments. And that may not be a good thing.

• *Wednesday 31 May* •

Try to pace yourself today, otherwise you could end up feeling exhausted and drained. You're very receptive to other people's emotions, which means you'll soak them up like a sponge, so try to steer clear of anyone who's negative or a right old misery guts. Keep a strong sense of your own self-worth, too, otherwise someone might sap your confidence.

JUNE AT A GLANCE

Love	♥ ♥
Money	£ $ £
Career	💻
Health	☼

• *Thursday 1 June* •

There's a lot of tension in the air today, thanks to the manipulative way that a certain person is behaving. What's come over them? Maybe they're worried about losing you and therefore they want to control you. Or perhaps you're the one who's being possessive because you're terrified of letting go of this person? Bear in mind that this may not be the most productive way to behave.

• *Friday 2 June* •

Today's New Moon is reminding you to think carefully about all you've learned in the past few weeks about your finances.

The coming fortnight is the time to take action, if that's what you think is needed, or perhaps you feel it would be better to sit tight and conserve your current savings. This is also a great opportunity to devote more hours in the week to the things that make your world go round.

● Saturday 3 June ●

The issues that erupted on Thursday rise to the surface again today, and this time they may be more difficult to deal with because they open up old emotional wounds or make you feel very vulnerable. If you're currently doing battle with that Taurean bugbear, possessiveness, you may feel that this is make-or-break time. Dare you allow more freedom and understanding into your relationship, or is that far too scary a prospect?

● Sunday 4 June ●

Is it true that you need a breather after the emotional angst of the past couple of days? Then give yourself a break today by doing something that you really enjoy and, preferably, in some light-hearted company. It may help to talk things through with a sympathetic friend but watch out for a tendency to hog the conversation – or your companion may start to suffer from compassion fatigue!

● Monday 5 June ●

Do you want to achieve a lot today? Then plan your strategy first, because that way you can make the most of your time and energy. It's an excellent day for taking part in a negotiation or discussion because you've got so much to contribute to the conversation. Not only are you a good listener now but you're also able to make some constructive suggestions.

• *Tuesday 6 June* •

Domestic matters are to the fore today, so try to spend some time at home or with members of the clan. These might be people who aren't related to you by blood but who are definitely family as far as you're concerned. It's a good day to go shopping for items that will increase the comfort or safety of your home. You'll also enjoy trying out a new type of food.

• *Wednesday 7 June* •

It's another domestic day, and you'll really get a kick out of pottering about within your own four walls. You might even hatch up some ambitious schemes that are calculated to improve your home in some way. Maybe you fancy changing the furniture around or you've spotted the very thing to give one of your rooms a new look. Food also plays an important role in your day.

• *Thursday 8 June* •

Someone wants to keep you under their thumb today, and they're not being very subtle about it. In fact, you may feel that you're shackled to them or that they think they own you, body and soul. Take care that you don't fall into this trap yourself, especially when you think about what happened at the start of the month. If you're going shopping you'll be attracted to something, but can you afford it?

• *Friday 9 June* •

There's a lot of tension with loved ones today. Someone may step out of line and try your patience, or feelings that you've buried may finally rise to the surface. Don't be surprised if a social event is marred or disrupted by the vexed question of money. It's certainly not wise to mix business and pleasure today, because they're completely incompatible.

• Saturday 10 June •

You know what they say about all work and no play. Not that you're in danger of becoming dull, but it certainly looks as if you need a break from the chores and duties that usually comprise your Saturdays. Besides, you're not really in the mood for them. Do something that gives your morale a boost while also allowing you to have a relaxing and enjoyable time.

• Sunday 11 June •

If you're thinking of going shopping today, you could come home with all sorts of items you didn't intend to buy. However, it's an especially good day to buy things that are a complete departure from your usual style, especially if they're really flattering and reveal a new aspect to your personality. If you're at work, you could encounter someone who sets your heart a-fluttering. What happens now?

• Monday 12 June •

There have been times recently when it's been hard to understand what a boss or superior expects from you, and unfortunately you experience another chapter of this long-running saga today. So listen carefully, or make sure this person puts their instructions in writing, so that you're covered in case things get nasty. It's the same story if you need to sort out some red tape – you may not get a straight answer.

• Tuesday 13 June •

It's another day when you need to keep alert if you're dealing with people in power. They may do things that take you by surprise, or they could change their mind about what they told you yesterday. If you're trying to meet a deadline or complete some complex paperwork, be prepared for lots of silly interruptions and distractions.

• *Wednesday 14 June* •

Someone's pulling a long face today, and they're doing it in your direction. Have you displeased them in some way or are you simply on the receiving end of their depressed or miserable mood? It's easy to absorb this or imagine that it's somehow your fault, but you may simply be in the wrong place at the wrong time. A partner isn't exactly a barrel of laughs, either. Sounds as though you're going to need your sense of humour!

• *Thursday 15 June* •

Watch out! A certain person is in the grip of a real power complex today, and it seems that you're getting the full brunt of it. They may boss you about or try to keep tabs on you, so you feel they won't allow you out of their sight. Yet if you're prepared to talk about this, you'll reach a deeper understanding of what each of you expects from the relationship.

• *Friday 16 June* •

Between now and the start of August is the perfect time to channel a lot of energy into your day-to-day life. You might do that by spending more time being sociable or you could decide to keep active and join a gym or athletics club. You'll be blessed with a lot of confidence when it comes to speaking up for yourself, which is just what you need if you're participating in discussions and negotiations.

• *Saturday 17 June* •

It's been quite a month as far as your close relationships are concerned. You've had to cope with possessiveness, jealousy and other emotional stresses, so let the current Full Moon help you to sort things out. Pretending that nothing's wrong will only prolong the agony, so it's much better to discuss your problems with the person concerned. Joint money matters may also need some tidying up.

• Sunday 18 June •

You're starting to feel very sociable, and you'll be in this gregarious mood for the next four weeks. It's a wonderful excuse to get together with some of your friends or to arrange a hectic social life. You'll certainly be very popular, so prepare to be in great demand. It's also a wonderful time to take off on a short break, such as an extended weekend, to somewhere beautiful or luxurious.

• Monday 19 June •

Today finds you in a very adventurous mood and eager to extract as much enjoyment from all your activities as possible. It's a great day for booking up a forthcoming holiday or arranging a long journey. You're also interested in expanding your knowledge of the world, perhaps by taking some formal lessons, reading an informative book or talking to someone who's absolutely fascinating.

• Tuesday 20 June •

Spare a thought for an older friend or relative who's going through a bad patch at the moment. Listen to their tale of woe, or let them know that you're thinking of them. Take care if you're expected to do a lot of work today because you'll find it hard to concentrate. Using your imagination will be a piece of cake, but poring over detailed facts and figures will be tough going.

• Wednesday 21 June •

Someone has a strong attraction for you today, but why? It could be because you both share an interest in something that you really value, or perhaps you're secretly drawn to what this person represents. Strange as it may seem, love could also blossom while you're sorting out a money matter. So if you're single, you'd better dash round to your bank or building society fast!

• *Thursday 22 June* •

The more sociable and outgoing you are today, the happier you'll be. It's definitely a day for getting out and about as much as possible, especially if you can be with friends and loved ones. If you've been wondering how to increase your social circle, think about joining a club or organization that caters for one of your interests. It's a good way to meet some like-minded people.

• *Friday 23 June* •

Communications start to go slightly haywire today, so take care. Gadgets and appliances, such as phones and computers, could go up the spout or messages may fail to reach their intended recipients. Be extra vigilant if you've got to send something important or valuable through the post, in case it goes missing. There's also the possibility of misunderstandings with other people, so choose your words carefully.

• *Saturday 24 June* •

Someone is in a delightfully expansive and jovial mood today, and you'll love being with them. They're a good laugh and they'll help you to relax and take life easy. Make the effort to meet new people because one of them could turn into a friend. You'll also enjoy spending time on a favourite hobby or pastime, especially if it lets your mind wander in whichever direction it cares to go.

● *Sunday 25 June* ●

Fancy a restful Sunday? Well, you may not get it because it seems that certain people are on the warpath. They may bite your head off or haul you over the coals for something that you thought was dead and buried. Alternatively, you're the one who takes offence at someone's thoughtless comment, or maybe you've been brooding over a past slight and now it's time to mention it?

● *Monday 26 June* ●

What is the day going to bring you? Anything that seems too restrictive or predictable will soon get you down, so try to do things that are interesting or unusual. If you've been getting fed up with your current job or you feel you've got too many responsibilities, start to think about how you can change things. You may not arrive at an overnight solution, but it won't hurt to put on your thinking cap.

● *Tuesday 27 June* ●

If you've fallen out with someone recently, this is your chance to talk about what's gone wrong and find an amicable solution. You may even end up laughing about everything and being much better friends than you were before. It's a great day for getting involved in community matters and local affairs, especially if you hope they're a passport to a revived social life.

● *Wednesday 28 June* ●

You're in a very serious mood, making it a great day to concentrate on subjects that require a lot of concentration and care. However, make sure that you don't become so wrapped up in such matters that you wear yourself out or start to feel depressed. Keep away from people who are coughing and sneezing, otherwise you'll easily pick up their germs.

• *Thursday 29 June* •

You're blessed with good humour and joviality today, so enjoy these feelings while they last. It's a terrific day for being with people who make you feel good, especially if you're all going out on the town or having fun in other ways. Sadly, if you're trying to follow a diet at the moment it will fly straight out of the window at the first opportunity, because you're not interested in stinting yourself. Try again tomorrow?

• *Friday 30 June* •

Jupiter, the planet of money, moves into the part of your chart that rules your personal finances today, and that spells good news for you. Over the next few months you can expect an increase in your cash flow, although it will be easy to get carried away by this and spend the money as soon as you've got it! Concentrating on your priorities in life will bring you lots of happiness and satisfaction, so find time for them.

JULY AT A GLANCE

Love	♥ ♥
Money	£ $
Career	💻
Health	☼

• *Saturday 1 July* •

Think about your daily routine over the next couple of weeks. Are you happy with it or could it do with livening up? If so, this is when you should swing into action. Even minor changes will make a difference. This is also a good time to have a serious chat with someone, especially if you need to iron out some problems between you or to reach an amicable solution.

• *Sunday 2 July* •

Someone is very charming and amenable today, making it easy for you to get on with them. You're also feeling very sociable and outgoing at the moment, and you'll enjoy meeting new people or getting together with old chums. If you need to say something important, you'll find just the words you were looking for and, what's more, you'll be the soul of discretion and tact.

• *Monday 3 July* •

Go carefully if you're at work or involved in an official business matter because there's plenty of scope for silly mistakes or misunderstandings. You may struggle to comprehend what someone is saying to you when they ramble on or keep contradicting themselves. Unfortunately it's not that much easier to fathom out a member of the family who's also being misleading at the moment.

• *Tuesday 4 July* •

Look after yourself today because it won't take much to make you feel depressed, vulnerable or inadequate. These unpleasant feelings may be provoked by someone who apparently disapproves of you or who keeps cutting you down to size. On the other hand, you may be miserable about circumstances that are currently afflicting your home or family life and which you feel powerless to prevent.

• *Wednesday 5 July* •

Let today be an antidote to yesterday's downbeat mood. So do something that you'll enjoy! One thing that will ensure you have a good time is going mad with your wallet or purse, especially if you can take a friend with you. You're interested in buying things that are luxurious, expensive or which make you feel wonderfully pampered.

• *Thursday 6 July* •

Good ideas will flow today, but it may not be easy to put them across. Maybe no one wants to listen to you or perhaps you find it difficult to marshal your thoughts. You may also get carried away and say far more than you meant to, so that everyone loses interest before you've finished. Alternatively, you could be the one who's stuck with someone who doesn't know when to shut up. Yawn!

• *Friday 7 July* •

You're in a very forceful and energetic mood today, enabling you to get a lot done. So don't let the grass grow under your feet! This is also a great day to fight your corner or defend your ideas, especially if you need to muster your courage before you speak out. However, watch for a slight tendency to fly off the handle or lose your temper with someone over a trifling matter.

• *Saturday 8 July* •

It's another day when tempers are short and people are ratty and irascible. You'll be especially irritated if you feel that someone is taking you for granted or playing you for a fool. You could also be annoyed with a colleague or client if you're at work. Do your best to concentrate whenever you handle anything sharp or hot, otherwise you could be slightly accident-prone.

• *Sunday 9 July* •

Dealings with women don't go quite according to plan today. For instance, someone may be competitive or imagine that they've got a rival. If you're trying to abide by some sensible health habits, such as forgetting that there's such a thing as chocolate, all your good resolutions may be forgotten today when your willpower deserts you and temptation takes over.

• *Monday 10 July* •

You're lost in a world of your own today, and that won't go down very well if you're supposed to pay attention to someone or do some complex work. You simply can't concentrate on anything for long, and you may even feel bored by the whole thing. However, using your imagination will pay dividends, so let your mind roam where it will and enjoy the journey!

• *Tuesday 11 July* •

Spend today getting to know someone better. You'll find it easy to establish a good rapport with them and you'll enjoy the in-depth conversation that will undoubtedly result. It's also a very good day for having a serious chat with someone that you know very well indeed, especially if certain problems need to be ironed out. Now's the time to get things off your chest and explain what's wrong.

• *Wednesday 12 July* •

Go carefully if you're involved in anything with financial or official overtones today because it won't always be easy to keep your mind on what's going on. Your thoughts may drift off to more interesting and exciting matters, especially if they happen to be your love life. It could also be difficult to remember someone's instructions or suggestions, especially if these are connected with red tape or bureaucracy, but do your best.

• *Thursday 13 July* •

Familiar faces and places have a lot of meaning for you between now and early August, making you reluctant to stray too far from your own front door. It's a great time to think about how to make your home even more comfy and cosy than it already is, especially if that means using your decorative skills in some way. It's also the perfect excuse for a big family party or a nostalgic get-together. How about it?

• Friday 14 July •

Take care with all official money matters today because there's plenty of room for mistakes. That may be because you're finding it hard to concentrate, but it's just as likely that these slip-ups aren't your fault. For instance, there could be a silly mistake in a bank statement or someone might give you the wrong information. Watch out for a loved one who gets the wrong end of the stick about something.

• Saturday 15 July •

It's a day for spending money, especially if you've decided to get cracking and start sprucing up your home. You'll love going round the shops, particularly if you take a loved one along for company. Take care if you're trying to conserve your cash because you're very tempted to splash out in all directions at the moment, and you know what that means!

• Sunday 16 July •

Today's Full Moon is going to give you a lot to think about over the coming fortnight. You may realize that matters aren't nearly as cut and dried as you thought. For instance, you may have to struggle over a moral dilemma or a question of principle, and discover that the answer isn't as easy as you'd hoped. Decisions connected with further education, travel or religion may also have to be thrashed out.

• Monday 17 July •

Thank goodness communications begin to return to the straight and narrow today, so things should soon start to flow smoothly again. Be wary about putting someone on a high pedestal at the moment because they could soon topple off and bring you a lot of disappointment. Will it be their fault for letting you down or your fault for imagining that they're superhuman in the first place?

• *Tuesday 18 July* •

It's hard to settle to anything rigorous, boring or routine today because you simply aren't in the mood. To make matters worse, there could be lots of interruptions whenever you do steel yourself to get down to some work, so you may end the day feeling that you've achieved precisely nothing. A boss or superior is a law unto themselves, making it almost impossible for you to understand what they expect from you. Maybe they don't know, either.

• *Wednesday 19 July* •

It's awfully easy to view things from a very gloomy perspective today. That may be because events are conspiring against you or simply because you can't muster up a lot of enthusiasm for anything at the moment. Try to take things gently whenever possible. You certainly shouldn't push yourself beyond your limits because you don't have the stamina right now. Watch out for a tendency to depression.

• *Thursday 20 July* •

What a delightfully lively and sociable day! You're in a very outgoing mood and are eager to get out and about as much as possible today. It all makes a lovely change from yesterday. You'll enjoy working on a favourite hobby or pastime, especially if it gives you time to think or it allows you to mix with some like-minded people. Speaking of which, if you don't have anything planned for the weekend, start arranging something now!

• *Friday 21 July* •

There's a very profound feeling in the air today, especially when it comes to your relationship with a certain someone. Maybe you're counting the minutes until you can be together again, or perhaps you've only just met and you're wondering if this person is going to be as important in your life as you suspect. Even if you've been with your other half for longer than either of you care to remember, there's an intensity between you today.

• *Saturday 22 July* •

The coming four weeks will find you very wrapped up in matters connected with your kith and kin. If you haven't seen some members of the family recently, now's your chance to put that to rights and arrange a get-together. You could also spend a lot of time thinking about the past, in which case your memories and recollections could give you some important messages about what's going on in your life at the moment.

• *Sunday 23 July* •

Someone's in a bit of a state today. They're likely to bite your head off as soon as look at you, and you may feel that you've got to tiptoe around on your best behaviour all day to avoid getting ticked off. However, even a chance remark may start a row, so maybe you should grab the chance to clear the air sooner rather than later. Unfortunately, you may also be feeling rather huffy. What's wrong?

• *Monday 24 July* •

It's another day when tensions are never far from the surface. Members of the family or someone that you know extremely well is likely to irritate the life out of you, and you may even decide that it's time to deliver a few home truths. That's fine, but avoid the temptation to start dragging up episodes from the past that have nothing to do with what's going on at the moment.

• Tuesday 25 July •

A woman isn't the easiest person in the world to deal with today. In fact, she may be downright difficult. You may also suspect that she's jealous or envious of you in some way, or perhaps she's competing with you for someone's affections. Even so, it's a lovely day for relaxing at home and taking life easy whenever you get the chance. You'll also enjoy doing some cooking, not to mention some eating!

• Wednesday 26 July •

Someone needs to be tucked under your protective wing today, so keep a look-out for lame ducks. It's a great day to go shopping, especially if you're on the hunt for a few treats or things to cheer yourself up. A loved one warms the cockles of your heart and reminds you that charity begins at home. If you've invited someone round to your place, you'll enjoy making a fuss of them.

• Thursday 27 July •

You're full of high hopes today, especially where your career and money are concerned. You could hear some wonderful news today, in which case you'll be doing handstands and heel clicks all over the place because what you hear is almost too good to be true. Take care if you're out spending money because it will flow through your fingers like sand.

• Friday 28 July •

It's another great day when you feel in a terrific mood, so make the most of it. Enjoy spending time with some of your nearest and dearest, especially if you can relax over a good meal or a convivial drink. It's also a good opportunity to buy something that brightens up your home or makes it more cosy. A loved one has some good news for you so keep your ears open.

● *Saturday 29 July* ●

You have a hankering for unusual people and places today, and anything or anyone that's too predictable or boring will soon turn you off. You may even be drawn to people who are usually a bit too racy or weird for your taste but who are just what the doctor ordered. Alternatively, you'll have to cope with a relative who wants to kick against the traces and is out to shock as many people as possible. And that includes you!

● *Sunday 30 July* ●

Someone is shooting from the hip today, able to say whatever they think. In fact, they may be rather abrupt or outspoken and you won't take very kindly to this. For instance, they could rise to the bait sooner than you realize what it is that you've said. Try to get out of the house at some point, otherwise you'll also start to feel agitated and restless, not to mention frustrated and rather irritable.

● *Monday 31 July* ●

You've been spending a lot of time on your home and family life over the past couple of weeks. Has this given you some food for thought? Maybe you've decided it's time to take the initiative in some way or turn over a new leaf. For instance, you could think about moving house or redoing the garden. You might also welcome a new face into the family over the next couple of weeks.

AUGUST AT A GLANCE

Love	♥ ♥ ♥ ♥ ♥
Money	£ $
Career	💻 💻 💻 💻
Health	☼ ☼ ☼ ☼

• *Tuesday 1 August* •

Channel your energies into your home and family life over the next six weeks, especially if you've got a long list of things that you want to achieve. You're raring to go and you're full of great ideas at the moment. All the same, watch out for a slight tendency at times to become very defensive or to imagine that people are out to get you and to react accordingly. You may find that they don't mean any harm at all.

• *Wednesday 2 August* •

Today you are in a very powerful position. You're feeling nicely confident and sure of yourself, especially if you need to sort out a potentially tricky or embarrassing situation. It's also a great day for having a serious talk with a member of the family or a close partner, particularly if you're prepared to dig below the surface and discuss things that are hush-hush, usually unspoken or often taboo.

• *Thursday 3 August* •

You're able to forge a deep link with a loved one today in which you can both try to understand one another better. If you've got some spare time you'll get lots of satisfaction from immersing yourself in a creative or artistic activity, particularly if it gives you some emotional solace at the same time. You may have to help a child or lover to understand an important lesson.

• *Friday 4 August* •

It's a great day for getting on well with the people around you, whether they're your family or your workmates. In fact, you've got a smile and a jolly word for everyone you meet today. Spare a thought for someone who's having a bit of a thin time of it at the moment or who isn't very well and needs your support. Maybe you could do some errands for them or cook them a meal?

• *Saturday 5 August* •

Getting along with others is as easy as falling off a log today. If you're at work, you'll enjoy being part of a team and making sure that everyone is OK. And if you're at home, you'll love making a fuss of someone and looking after their every need. If you don't always see eye-to-eye with someone, this is a great opportunity to sit down with them and find some common ground.

• *Sunday 6 August* •

Your love life starts to blossom from today, and it will continue to flourish for the rest of the month. This is your chance to immerse yourself in activities that you enjoy, particularly if they bring out your creative talents or allow you to express your true self. All loving relationships will go well now, whether they're platonic or passionate, and if you're currently single you might end the month as part of a happy couple. Sounds good!

• *Monday 7 August* •

Memories of the past will never be far from your thoughts during the next two weeks, and you could also have some very strong and powerful dreams. What are these trying to tell you? Take note of your dreams, and of any strong memories that float into your mind, because they could carry important messages about what's going on in your life at the moment. They may also help you to resolve long-standing emotional blocks.

• Tuesday 8 August •

Get set for a rather tricky day, especially when you're dealing with people in authority. You may have to cope with someone who apparently doesn't know what on earth they're doing and who creates havoc all around. You may also have to account for something that you did in the past and which now comes back to haunt you. It will be wiser to face the music than to fudge the issue.

• Wednesday 9 August •

It's another day when it's hard to handle bosses and superiors. Today, it's because someone may not be telling the truth or they may be in a state of total confusion. Someone may say one thing and do another, or they could twist the facts to suit themselves. Try to avoid agreeing to anything legal or binding today because you may not be in full possession of the facts.

• Thursday 10 August •

Try to be sensible and practical with your cash over the next couple of months. It's not a good time to fritter it away or throw it around, and you may feel uncomfortable if you start doing this. Instead, this is a great opportunity to investigate any schemes or arrangements that will help you to capitalize on your money, whether you're rolling in it or you're as poor as a church mouse.

• Friday 11 August •

There's a very restless feeling in the air today, and it's affecting your home and career. You could have to deal with someone who's feeling bored or restless, and who wants to ginger things up by being shocking or disruptive. They may even announce some startling changes or revolutionary plans. Do they mean what they say or are they simply trying to wind you up? Wait and see.

• *Saturday 12 August* •

Are you happy with your current home life or are you longing to introduce some changes? If you know that you need to alter your existing set-up in some way, today is a perfect opportunity to think through your plans. Even better if you can discuss them with the other people concerned, or you can bounce your ideas off a friend. If you need to sort out a domestic bill or account, get cracking today.

• *Sunday 13 August* •

Take care if you're going anywhere near the shops today because it will be awfully easy to spend, spend, spend. In fact, you could get quite carried away! You'll love bringing home lots of trophies, especially if they're luxurious or extravagant, but you may not feel quite so chuffed once you've worked out what they cost! The loving and enthusiastic behaviour of a certain person will really make your day.

• *Monday 14 August* •

Beware of any hint of jealousy or possessiveness today because it will leave a nasty taste in your mouth. A partner may try to impose emotional rules or restrictions on you, or they could use money or sex to manipulate you. It's not a good day to enter into any form of financial partnership, because someone may have a hidden agenda that you know nothing about at the moment.

• *Tuesday 15 August* •

Today's Full Moon is focusing your attention on your career and your long-term goals and ambitions. Over the coming fortnight you need to think carefully about whether everything is heading along the right lines or whether you should make some timely adjustments. It's an excellent time to meet an important deadline or finish off a project, especially if you hope that all this hard work will bring you some good rewards.

• Wednesday 16 August •

Are you happy with a close relationship, or are you aware that it's time to make a few changes? The underlying atmosphere at the moment is reminding you that every relationship needs to keep changing because otherwise it can stagnate. So be prepared now to introduce some constructive and positive changes that will breathe new life into your partnership and also enable you to work together to overcome any problems that are currently besetting you.

• Thursday 17 August •

Friends play an important role in your life today, and you could feel a very strong bond with one chum in particular. They might do you a good turn or you may simply enjoy their company. If you haven't got anything planned for the weekend, try to get something organized today even if it's only very minor. You'll enjoy having something to look forward to!

• Friday 18 August •

If you've been waiting for a payment to arrive but it's long overdue, you could heave a huge sigh of relief today when it finally lands on the mat or is pressed into your hand. You could also hear some good news if you're currently applying for a government benefit or allowance. It's a great day for buying something that will boost your morale or bring you a lot of pleasure, and it doesn't have to cost an arm and a leg, either!

• *Saturday 19 August* •

You're feeling nicely enthusiastic and energetic today, so what have you got planned? You may be in the mood to get busy about the house, perhaps because you fancy doing some cleaning or DIY. Or maybe you'd rather be working in the garden? If you've been nerving yourself up to mention a potentially difficult topic, this is a good day to square your shoulders and start talking. You'll be fine.

• *Sunday 20 August* •

There have been times recently when it's been difficult to deal with certain emotional problems, especially if you've felt that they've controlled you rather than the other way round. But all that starts to become a little easier from today, thank goodness. There could also be a few changes to your finances, especially if you share them with others. In fact, this is the ideal day to reach an important decision connected with a joint account.

• *Monday 21 August* •

There's a delightfully easy-going feeling in the air today, and you're in the mood to enjoy yourself. Yes, it may be Monday but you certainly don't have any Monday blues! Quite the opposite, in fact, because you-know-who may say or do something that really makes your day. It's also a lovely excuse to treat yourself to something luxurious or morale-boosting.

• *Tuesday 22 August* •

The astrological accent is firmly placed on your love life from today, and you've got plenty of time in which to really let your hair down and have some fun. Introduce love, laughter and happiness into your life, especially if that means spending time with some of your favourite people or seeking out activities that always make you feel on top of the world. Life is for living now, so throw yourself into it head first!

• *Wednesday 23 August* •

Even though you're all set to have some fun, there's a rather sobering influence at work today. You may feel constrained or held back by someone's miserable mood, or you could be suddenly brought up short by a lack of money. Speaking of which, it's not a good day for being extravagant because, even if you enjoy yourself at the time, you'll soon start to worry whether you did the right thing.

• *Thursday 24 August* •

It's another day when money – or the lack of it – nags away at you. You may be feeling the pinch, even though you've got your eye on something that you long to buy, or you may feel bad because you can't afford to look after a loved one in the way you'd like. Show them you care in other ways, perhaps by telling them how much they mean to you.

• *Friday 25 August* •

It's another lovely day when you find it easy to get on well with others. In fact, you'll be far happier when you're with other people than when you're alone. If you've been having problems with someone recently, this is a great day to have a gentle chat with them. Breaking the ice or sharing a joke will help you to get things back on an even keel.

• *Saturday 26 August* •

Relax and enjoy yourself today. As if you needed any persuading! You're in the mood to spend time with people who occupy a special place in your heart. You're also feeling quite playful, so you'll love being with a child or playing with a pet. Something else you'll enjoy is visiting a place of beauty, especially if it gets you out of the house and allows you to have a mini-holiday.

• Sunday 27 August •

Trying to make someone change their mind? Then give it a miss today because you'll simply be wasting your breath. This person is determined to stand their ground, whether it's in their best interests or not. Watch out, too, for someone who's in a rather suspicious mood and who may even accuse you of stepping out of line or misbehaving. Are they imagining things or are they on to something?

• Monday 28 August •

There's a very disruptive atmosphere today, making it difficult for you to settle to anything for long. You might be interrupted every time you've got down to some work, or you could have to cope with someone who keeps changing their mind about what they want. Your best bet is to go with the flow and be as flexible as possible, otherwise you'll soon feel exhausted and scratchy.

• Tuesday 29 August •

Mind how you go today, especially when dealing with people in authority. You may encounter someone who's determined to go their own way or be a thorn in everyone's side. They could also stir up trouble simply to see what happens next. Keep out of their way or try to jolly them out of their unruly mood. By the way, it's not a good day to sign an agreement or contract.

• Wednesday 30 August •

There's been a strong focus on your social and emotional life over the past few weeks, and the current New Moon is telling you to marshal your thoughts and see if you need to make any changes. The coming fortnight is a fabulous time to get a new relationship off the ground, and you could also be bowled over by someone's affection for you. There could be great news about a baby or child.

• *Thursday 31 August* •

You take great delight and pleasure in being of service to people over the next three weeks, whether you do so for love or money. If your job involves beauty or fashion, things will go very well for you now. Whatever you do for a living, this is a good time to improve your relationships with your colleagues or to apply for a new job. Your charm will stand you in excellent stead!

SEPTEMBER AT A GLANCE

Love	♥ ♥ ♥ ♥
Money	£ $
Career	💻 💻 💻 💻
Health	☼ ☼ ☼ ☼ ☼

• *Friday 1 September* •

You're in a very lively mood today and you have no interest in doing things that are boring, predictable or run of the mill. For once, you'd rather branch out in a new direction or do something for the first time rather than the hundredth. Try to give yourself frequent breaks if you're at work, otherwise your attention span will dwindle away to nothing. A colleague may have a surprise for you.

• *Saturday 2 September* •

Money has a funny habit of vanishing. In fact, you may even suspect that it evaporates as soon as you hold it in your hand, and by the end of the day you could have spent quite a tidy sum. That's fine if you've got it to spare, but watch out if you're supposed to be following a budget. A loved one is carried away by enthusiasm today, but do you think they're protesting too much?

• Sunday 3 September •

If someone does you a favour today you'll be tremendously grateful and extremely delighted. You may even feel that this person has acted above and beyond the call of duty. If your job involves being of service to others, you have a strong need to do your very best today, and you'll willingly do what you can to help. If it's your day of rest, relax and give yourself a complete breather.

• Monday 4 September •

Very powerful influences are at work today, especially where your finances are concerned. If you're thinking of applying for a loan or some other fiscal favour, make very sure that you know what you're doing. If in doubt, bide your time. Watch out for someone who may try to use their money or power to steal a march on you or coerce you into doing what they want. Above all, don't behave this way yourself!

• Tuesday 5 September •

Love may make the world go round but it also has a nasty habit of making it grind to a halt at times, and your world certainly undergoes a mini-wobble today. It seems that the trouble stems from a loved one who's being difficult, possessive or who wants to boss you about. If this is an old, old story, you'll probably waste no time in telling this person exactly what you think of them. The sooner you do that, the sooner things can return to normal.

• Wednesday 6 September •

It's another day when tempers are hasty and people are likely to fly off the handle. You may blurt out your feelings in a fit of pique or simply because you've been provoked to your very limits. However, bear in mind that this person may be feeling vulnerable or on the defensive, and that a little tender loving care could make all the difference to their mood – and, therefore, to yours.

• *Thursday 7 September* •

Get set for a bout of hard work! You're going to be kept pretty busy this month, especially on the job front. You might have to fill in for someone who's on holiday or who's ill, or there may be other reasons why you have to do more than your fair share. It's a marvellous time to think about your work situation and whether you're happy with it. If not, talk to someone who can help, or start scanning the Situations Vacant columns in the paper.

• *Friday 8 September* •

It's been a bit of a fraught week at times, but thank goodness you end it on a high note. You'll benefit from someone's kindness or generosity, and they could even do you the sort of favour that money can't buy. Speaking of money, it's a marvellous day for investing in items that will boost your health or fitness, or make you feel like a million dollars. So what are you going to buy?

• *Saturday 9 September* •

Go carefully if you're at work today because you keep drifting off into a little world of your own. That means it will be difficult to keep track of what other people are talking about, and it will be a real effort to concentrate on anything that involves complex or detailed work. Using your imagination, however, is a piece of cake, so let it run free and then you'll hatch some great ideas.

• *Sunday 10 September* •

You're in a very imaginative and inspired frame of mind today, so jot down your thoughts as they come to you. Even if you can't put your ideas into action immediately, they could come in handy over the next few months. There's a lot of kindness in the air today, whether you're on the receiving end or you're helping other people. Be prepared to give someone the benefit of the doubt if you're unsure of them.

• *Monday 11 September* •

Someone's a bit quick off the mark today, especially when it comes to work. They may behave in rather rash or hasty ways, and it will be no surprise if these cause more problems than they solve. Try to pace yourself if you start to feel restless or agitated, because that means you're likely to rush in where angels fear to tread. A boss or superior is operating on a short fuse, so keep away.

• *Tuesday 12 September* •

Money matters start to slow down from today, and there could be delays to payments over the next few weeks. It certainly isn't a good idea to spend money that you haven't got at the moment, so keep a close eye on those credit card bills and, if necessary, do a bit of juggling to ensure you're paying the lowest possible rate of interest. A financial deal might get snarled up now, so patience is needed.

• *Wednesday 13 September* •

Spend some time during the coming fortnight thinking about your hopes and wishes for the future. How are they coming along? Is everything hunky-dory or are you wondering if you're barking up the wrong tree? This is the ideal time to make any adjustments necessary, whether they're large or small. You may have to reach an important decision about a friend.

• *Thursday 14 September* •

Does your job give you enough mental and emotional satisfaction? Does it bring you into contact with interesting people or do you often feel like climbing the walls through sheer frustration? If you're longing for a change of job, start thinking about what you can do. Don't be surprised if your working routine introduces you to an attractive someone who has a dazzling and magnetic effect on you.

• *Friday 15 September* •

Even though Taureans aren't afraid of hard work, you simply aren't in the mood for it today. You'd much rather take things easy and relax. In fact, it may even be quite an effort for you to summon up the energy to do anything exacting or strenuous. If you're currently trying to abide by a diet, your willpower could desert you at the first whiff of whatever is your calorific downfall. Oh well, there's always tomorrow!

• *Saturday 16 September* •

It's a great day for keeping busy at home, especially if you've got a long list of things that need to be done. You'll enjoy rolling up your sleeves and getting on with things, especially when you can survey everything you've achieved. Even better if you can rope in other members of the family to help you. If you need to raise a subject that's got the potential to be embarrassing or tricky, you're feeling brave enough to do it today.

• *Sunday 17 September* •

Life is what you make it between now and early November, and you're keen to make it as good as possible. Make the most of the dynamic energy that starts to surge through you from today, because it will carry you a long way and give you plenty of oomph. Your love life could become quite hectic too, because this promises to be a very ardent and amorous time. If you're single at the moment, you may not stay that way for long!

• Monday 18 September •

Take care because today threatens to be rather frustrating. You might feel that you're beating your head against a brick wall as far as a certain person is concerned, or you could have to deal with someone who blocks all your suggestions and ideas. Channel your frustrations into something constructive and therapeutic, so you've got an achievement to show for the day after all.

• Tuesday 19 September •

The more inventive and original you are today, the more you'll enjoy yourself. So it's not a day for being traditional or conventional, even though that may not be easy for you if you're a typical Taurean. If you've been struggling with a long-term problem, approaching it from a different angle may help you to view it from a new perspective and, with luck, to see the way forward.

• Wednesday 20 September •

It's easy to get on well with other people today because you're in such a light-hearted mood. This is a great opportunity to get to know someone better, especially if you work with them. It's also a good day for buying something that will boost your health or well-being, such as some vitamin supplements or some nutritious food. Try to find an opportunity to put your feet up and take it easy.

• Thursday 21 September •

A close relationship could cause you a few headaches today, thanks to the difficult behaviour of a certain someone. Any tension or stress that has been simmering away under the surface will finally come to light, probably erupting in a row or showdown. If you're wise you'll try to keep money and friends as far apart as possible. They simply don't mix at the moment.

• Friday 22 September •

The Sun moves signs today and begins to influence your working environment and your well-being. This means that over the coming four weeks you'll gain a lot of satisfaction from your work, and also from being of service to others. If you're not happy with your current job, start thinking about what you can do instead. This is also a good time to look after your health, so take care of yourself.

• Saturday 23 September •

You're in the mood to get on with a lot of hard work today, whether it involves your job or your personal life. If you want to make the most of the day, plan what you're going to do in advance so you don't waste time or energy. You're also feeling quite thrifty now, so it's an excellent opportunity to go shopping for bargains or to begin a new savings scheme.

• Sunday 24 September •

Relationships promise to flourish during the next four weeks because you're keen to get on well with everyone you encounter. It's a great time for negotiations and discussions, thanks to your need for harmony, but try not to agree on things simply for the sake of peace. There may be times when it would be better to stand up for yourself, even if that does mean causing a heated debate!

• Monday 25 September •

You start the week in cracking good form, brimming with energy and full of good ideas. You're also feeling very sociable, so if you can't get out today at least you can arrange something for later in the week. A child or pet will keep you on your toes now, but you'll thoroughly enjoy rushing around after them. A loved one could react in a slightly hasty way, so be prepared for a rise in the emotional temperature.

• *Tuesday 26 September* •

You take tremendous pride in helping others today, whether it's expected of you or not. If your job involves taking care of others, you could find yourself in the limelight or you might receive a nice pat on the back. If you're currently experiencing problems, try to confide in someone whose opinion you trust and who can give you some good advice.

• *Wednesday 27 September* •

Someone isn't being very realistic today. They may have their head in the clouds or they could allow their imagination to run away with them. If this sounds like you, try to keep your feet on the ground, otherwise you'll come down to earth with a nasty bump when reality finally intrudes on your thoughts. Go carefully if it's a boss or superior who's indulging in some wishful thinking.

• *Thursday 28 September* •

Talking to partners is the best way to make an impact on them during the next two months. Discussing any difficulties that arise and working together to find a solution will help a relationship to go from strength to strength, and also allow each of you to have your say. This is a marvellous time to take part in discussions because you're eager to put your ideas forward but you're also happy to listen to other people's views.

• *Friday 29 September* •

If someone has made you some promises recently, you may have a long wait before these start to materialize. In fact, you should keep a hefty pinch of salt handy from today, ready for those times when people promise things that they can't deliver. You also need to keep careful control over your finances now, because it's not the right time to overspend or gamble with your money.

• *Saturday 30 September* •

It's a delight to be with a certain someone today, and they feel the same way about you! Harmony reigns, in fact. This is really good news if you've fallen out with you-know-who and you're hoping that you can start to patch up your quarrel. Maybe you should make the first move now, or at least let this person know that you're willing to talk about what went wrong. If you're going out on the town with someone, you'll have a wonderful time.

OCTOBER AT A GLANCE

Love	♥ ♥ ♥ ♥ ♥
Money	£ $ £
Career	💻 💻
Health	☼ ☼

• *Sunday 1 October* •

Be careful about who you trust today because some people may not be telling you the whole story. This could be because they're feeling forgetful or it might be for more nefarious reasons. It's certainly not a good day for signing on any dotted lines or reaching verbal agreements, especially if a lot is at stake or you suspect you may want to change your mind at a later date.

• *Monday 2 October* •

There's plenty of charm in the air today, as you'll discover when you encounter a certain someone. If you meet them for the first time now, you'll be very intrigued and attracted by them. Will this be the start of something big or will you be ships that pass in the night? It's also a great day for improving your relationship with you-know-who, so bend over backwards to find a happy medium with them.

• *Tuesday 3 October* •

The events that take place today make you realize that you need to introduce some important changes to a close liaison. However, you may find that your other half isn't interested or might even be determined to oppose you. There could also be problems connected with someone's power complex or their urge to tell you what to do. You don't like it but you may feel unable to retaliate.

• *Wednesday 4 October* •

Life is full of promise and enjoyment today, so you'll need no prompting to make the most of it. It's surprisingly easy to get on well with colleagues, even if you aren't usually bosom buddies. Use this opportunity to forge a deeper understanding with them, or simply work hard to make them laugh. In fact, humour is your passport to getting on well with others now.

• *Thursday 5 October* •

Yesterday you were laughing but you're not feeling quite so happy today. What's wrong? You may not have as much energy as you'd like, or your confidence could be dented by someone's thoughtless comments. You may also be itching to give a certain person a few home truths, especially if they've tested your patience recently and it's now wearing paper-thin.

• *Friday 6 October* •

Concentrate on ways of boosting your income or making more of your money today. You might decide to ask someone's financial advice, or perhaps you feel confident enough to make some decisions on your own. It's also an excellent day for concentrating on your career and public status, especially if you're working on something that carries a lot of meaning for you.

• *Saturday 7 October* •

It's another day when tempers are short, so take care. Today, you've got to deal with someone who easily flies off the handle or who bites your head off given the smallest opportunity. What's eating them? Alternatively, you're the one who's feeling waspish and who lashes out in all directions. Work off your excess nervous energy by doing something enjoyable and therapeutic.

• *Sunday 8 October* •

Your usual Sunday routine palls today, so try to arrange to do something different. Otherwise, you'll soon feel restless and edgy, making it hard to settle to anything for long. If you're getting together with the family, don't be surprised if one of the clan behaves in ways that raise eyebrows all round or that go completely against the grain. What's got into them?

• *Monday 9 October* •

You're not in a very cheerful mood today, so take things gently whenever you get the chance. You may receive some depressing news about your finances or you might realize that there isn't as much money to throw around as you'd thought. As a result, something that you were looking forward to may have to be scaled down or even postponed for the time being.

• *Tuesday 10 October* •

The more original and inventive you are today, the more you'll enjoy yourself. Be prepared to branch out in a new direction or do something for the first time. If you've been thinking about making changes to your job or career, this is an excellent opportunity to take things one step further. Perhaps now's the time to apply for that new job or break out on your own and become self-employed?

• *Wednesday 11 October* •

You're the height of popularity today so you can expect plenty of invitations to come your way. And if none arrive, then why not issue a few of your own? It's a great day for breaking the ice with someone or inviting them out, especially if you've got romantic designs on them. A friend or partner is kind or good-hearted, and you'll really enjoy their company.

• *Thursday 12 October* •

It's one of those days when you feel slightly dreamy. You'll enjoy drifting off into a little reverie or curling up with a good book and letting the rest of the world pass you by. You could also find yourself lending a sympathetic ear to someone's tale of woe or giving them some carefully considered advice. If you're involved in a charity or good cause, it will go well today.

• *Friday 13 October* •

Are you superstitious about the date? If so, you'd be wise to avoid getting involved in any financial deals because you will meet a tough opponent. Even so, there could be an emotional tug of war with a certain person in which neither of you is prepared to back down. Both of you may believe that you're right and that it's up to the other person to capitulate. It's a great day for making changes to a relationship, but these may not be greeted with much enthusiasm.

• Saturday 14 October •

Spend time over the coming fortnight thinking carefully about the fears and anxieties that are nagging away at the back of your mind. If you've allowed them to dominate your thoughts recently, the current Full Moon is giving you the opportunity to lay them finally to rest. Be prepared to face up to what's worrying you, because that's the first step towards sorting out the problem.

• Sunday 15 October •

Vagueness and confusion have coloured your career recently, making you unsure of where you're going. You may also have lost direction and enthusiasm about long-term goals, but from today you'll start to regain your impetus. A secret could come to light now, in which case it will have an important bearing on your sense of self-esteem and confidence.

• Monday 16 October •

Personal projects begin to grind to a halt today and it could be hard to get things moving again for the next few weeks. You may lose interest in something for a while, or you might have to put it on the back burner while you concentrate on other priorities. Take care of yourself during the rest of the year because you won't always have as much stamina and energy as you'd like.

• Tuesday 17 October •

If you're going shopping, don't be surprised if you bring home a few purchases that you wouldn't normally buy. Today, however, you simply can't resist them! It's a great day for sorting out important money matters, especially if you approach them from a slightly unconventional angle. You may also deal with an official or bureaucrat who's a real breath of fresh air.

• *Wednesday 18 October* •

Recently you've been finding it easy to talk to partners and say what you think, but communications start to become rather snarled up from today. Be very careful about agreeing to things now – it may be difficult to back down at a later date if you change your mind. It's important to choose your words carefully when talking to partners to avoid misunderstandings and disagreements.

• *Thursday 19 October* •

Your emotions take a very intense turn from today, and they'll stay that way for the next four weeks. It's a wonderful opportunity to explore how you feel about a certain someone, especially if that means letting your actions speak louder than words. It's certainly a very ardent and sexy time, and if you're single at the moment you could soon meet someone who has a powerful impact on you.

• *Friday 20 October* •

You could feel taken for granted or unappreciated today, and you won't like that one bit. For instance, you might lend someone a hand but receive little thanks, or you could put yourself out for a certain person and then wonder why you bothered. If you're at work, you might lose your temper with someone who is rude or unappreciative. But beware of making a big fuss about nothing.

• *Saturday 21 October* •

It's very tempting to fly off the handle and bite someone's head off today. You may even do it before you've realized what you've said, because your reactions are very emotional and very fast. Watch out for a member of the family who's feeling bitter or resentful because they don't care who knows it. You could soon feel the sharp edge of their tongue.

• Sunday 22 October •

Thank goodness today looks much easier than the past couple of days. In fact, you're feeling very easy-going and you're keen to get on well with everyone you meet. This is the perfect opportunity to soothe someone's ruffled feathers by giving them some tender loving care. There could also be a romantic encounter with someone who's in a position of power and influence. It will set hearts a-flutter!

• Monday 23 October •

You have a strong need to be with other people over the next four weeks. In fact, you might even feel like a fish out of water if you have to spend too much time on your own. It's a marvellous time to enter into a partnership with someone, whether you do it for business or pleasure. You'll also find that teamwork is your best bet now, and you'll really enjoy being part of the gang.

• Tuesday 24 October •

You get the chance to forge a strong emotional bond with a special person today, especially if you're prepared to talk about your deep feelings. If you've fallen out with someone recently, this is a good opportunity to set matters to rights. It's also a great day for working on a creative or artistic project, especially if it helps you to relax and unwind.

• Wednesday 25 October •

Making the effort to get on well with colleagues and customers will repay you in many ways today. For a start, you'll enjoy the harmonious atmosphere that results from your actions. You could also discover the hidden side to a certain someone, and this might make you very attracted to them. There could also be a little windfall, bonus or tip for you.

• *Thursday 26 October* •

It's very difficult to understand what a certain person expects from you today. What's more, they may not have much idea themselves, because it's highly likely that they're in a bit of a fog at the moment. It's not a good day for reaching any important decisions because you may not be aware of all the facts. You might also keep changing your mind.

• *Friday 27 October* •

Today's New Moon is reminding you that partnerships are of paramount importance at the moment. If you're going to get hitched to someone or set up home with them over the next fortnight, you couldn't have chosen a more auspicious time in the whole year. Congratulations! This is also a good opportunity to repair a rift with someone and get things back on an even keel.

• *Saturday 28 October* •

Your emotions have a very intense flavour today. That's wonderful if you're currently involved in a passionate or emotional relationship because you'll be able to immerse yourself in it to the exclusion of all else. You might even find that love transforms your life in some way now, whether it happens through circumstances around you or you undergo some inner, psychological changes.

• *Sunday 29 October* •

It's not easy to get on well with a certain someone today. They're stand-offish, distant or they keep criticizing you. To make matters worse, you're feeling quite lonely, and you may imagine that people are out to get you. Try to do something that will boost your morale and confidence. Keep away from people who are coughing and spluttering, otherwise you could catch their germs.

• *Monday 30 October* •

You're in a very chatty mood today, and you'll really enjoy talking to whoever happens to be around. It's a good day for getting involved in a discussion or negotiation because you'll enjoy the cut and thrust of a lively verbal exchange. A partner or friend is also feeling very voluble, as you'll discover when they almost talk your ears off.

• *Tuesday 31 October* •

Love and money go together like oil and water today so try to keep them at arm's length whenever you get the chance. Someone might feel jealous of something you've got, or they could use money in an attempt to control you. Feelings are also running high now, and a loved one might lose their temper or get into a paddy over something they feel strongly about.

NOVEMBER AT A GLANCE

Love	♥ ♥ ♥ ♥ ♥
Money	£ $
Career	💻 💻 💻
Health	☼ ☼ ☼

• *Wednesday 1 November* •

There's a certain amount of confusion in the air today. People may say one thing and do another, or you could receive misleading advice when you ask someone's opinion. Play safe by avoiding any sort of legal or binding agreement – you may not be in full possession of the facts. You could also be confronted by the results of some actions that you hoped everyone had forgotten about. Not so, it seems.

• *Thursday 2 November* •

It's a day for getting things done, so make the most of today's burst of energy and discipline. You're in a very businesslike mood, and you're determined to achieve whatever you set out to do. It's an especially good day for working on a creative or artistic project, or anything else that allows you to express your true talents. Establish a constructive relationship with a loved one.

• *Friday 3 November* •

You're in a dynamic and go-getting mood again, and today you're also feeling quite adventurous. So it's a great opportunity to spread your wings and explore something new. A loved one could have a suggestion for you that seems quite daring and challenging, but you can't resist taking them up on their offer! If you haven't got anything planned for the weekend, arrange to visit somewhere you've never been before.

• *Saturday 4 November* •

You start to channel a lot of energy into your working life from today, and you won't let up until just before Christmas. This is the perfect opportunity to show colleagues and clients that you've got what it takes, especially if you've felt the need to prove yourself lately. It's also an excellent time to take charge of your health. If you know you don't take enough exercise, this is when you should begin. But start gently!

• *Sunday 5 November* •

You're in a rather sombre mood today. You may feel weighed down by responsibilities and duties that you can't wriggle out of, or you could become deflated when you're on the receiving end of someone's miserable mood. Personal plans may have to be put on hold when other commitments get in the way, and you may feel that you've got to like it or lump it.

• *Monday 6 November* •

Thank goodness yesterday's rather morose mood has vanished, leaving you cheerful and back on form. In fact, you're feeling rather extravagant today, so take care if you're passing any shops because you could easily give in to some impulsive spending sprees. If you've got the money to spare, you'll enjoy buying something connected with a favourite hobby or interest.

• *Tuesday 7 November* •

Hold tight today because communications could go haywire when dealing with workmates and customers. Someone may get the wrong end of the stick or they could get into a terrible muddle when handling paperwork or using a computer. Double-check the arrangements if you're attending a medical appointment today – someone may have got the time or the date wrong. There might also be long delays.

• *Wednesday 8 November* •

Thank heavens your communications begin to return to normal from today. You've been coping with all sorts of mix-ups and muddles over the past three weeks, but now you get the chance to unravel the problems and sort out what went wrong. If you need to make a decision about a partnership or a certain person, this is the ideal day to do it, provided you're sure of your ground.

• *Thursday 9 November* •

Strong feelings of restlessness steal over you today, making it hard to settle to anything for long. You'll feel especially edgy when working on things that are important, bureaucratic or bristling with regulations. Take care that your rebellious mood doesn't upset the apple cart or earn the disapproval of someone who could make life difficult for you. Let off steam in productive ways.

• *Friday 10 November* •

It's a day for making plans, especially if you want to progress in your work or your public reputation. Decide what you want to achieve and how you're going to go about it. It's also an excellent day for rolling up your sleeves and showing certain people what you're capable of. You're an invaluable member of any team now.

• *Saturday 11 November* •

Today's Full Moon is reminding you that it's time to examine your personal life in great detail. Be prepared to sort out the wheat from the chaff, by drawing a line under any activities or arrangements that aren't working out in the way you'd like. If you're brave enough to cut your losses, you can start again, confident in the knowledge that you will be making much better use of your time and energy.

• *Sunday 12 November* •

Start as you mean to go on by thinking carefully about what you want to achieve over the next few months. Map out a strategy if you like, or work things out in your head. You're in a very practical and methodical mood today, so you won't waste your time on anything that's frivolous or unproductive. Give yourself a breather at some point and do something relaxing.

• *Monday 13 November* •

Life is full of adventure from today and it will stay that way until early December. It's a wonderful time for finding ways of expanding your horizons, whether you do that mentally or physically. You're certainly in the mood for an adventure, and if you can combine that with some love and romance then so much the better! Someone from another country or walk of life will make a massive impression on you.

• *Tuesday 14 November* •

Whatever you've planned to do today, hard work doesn't come into the equation. You simply aren't interested in anything that looks or feels like a lot of slog, but that could cause problems if you're expected to pull your finger out. Get the chores over as soon as possible and then devote yourself to having fun. You're especially attracted to anything with cosmopolitan overtones.

• *Wednesday 15 November* •

You've had to deal with a lot of confusion and some strange complications during the past six weeks, but you finally get the chance to sort things out today. Even so, it may be difficult to know exactly what went wrong, perhaps because someone keeps changing their story or they're hard to pin down. It's important to abide by the truth today, even if you *are* tempted to tell a little white lie. You'll be caught out if you do!

• *Thursday 16 November* •

You're fired up with enthusiasm today, making you deter-mined to get a lot done. It's an especially good day for getting on with your work, and you'll enjoy ticking off lots of items on your list of things to do. It's also a good day for sorting out a money matter. If you think it's about time you started to improve your health, consider joining a gym or going for a swim.

• *Friday 17 November* •

It's difficult to get very far when talking to a certain someone today. You may feel that you're going round in circles with them or that they don't seem to know what day it is. Be very careful if this person happens to be in charge of you or if they have a lot of clout. You don't have a lot of energy, so you should pace yourself whenever possible.

• *Saturday 18 November* •

Take care because it's difficult to get on well with other people today. They could be scratchy or unpleasant, or you may feel impatient with them. Things are especially tense when you're with people you know very well, so watch out when talking to loved ones or your partner. Something that's been rankling for some time could finally get the better of you, making you blow your top. And about time too?

• *Sunday 19 November* •

It's another difficult day, but this time you're feeling lonely and isolated from the people around you. Someone could give you the cold shoulder or freeze you out if they don't agree with what you're doing, or maybe you're not in a very chatty mood yourself. Unfortunately it's easy to imagine that things are worse than they really are, but try not to sink into a slough of despond. Are things really that bad?

• *Monday 20 November* •

Thank goodness the sun comes out again for you today, making you feel much more cheerful than you've been in the past few days. For a start, you get the chance to patch up your quarrel if you fell out with someone, and you're also feeling a lot more optimistic. Why not celebrate by doing something enjoyable or buying a treat for you and your other half?

• *Tuesday 21 November* •

You're in a very outgoing mood today, so you won't be happy if you have to spend too much time by yourself. You also won't be very chuffed if work commitments interfere with your social life, because you'd much rather go out on the town than spend time slogging over a hot computer. If you've got itchy feet, why not arrange a weekend break so you've got something to look forward to?

• *Wednesday 22 November* •

It's another day when you're feeling restless and you aren't keen on doing too much hard work. Someone you encounter today has a galvanizing effect on you. They could make you go all tingly because you're so attracted to them, or they might have a different effect on you and make you feel angry and irritable. Either way, they make a big impression on you.

• *Thursday 23 November* •

Take care when talking to people in authority today because it may be difficult to keep track of your thoughts. Your mind may keep wandering off on to other subjects, so it's hard to pay attention to what's going on around you. If you're doing something that requires a lot of concentration, try to double-check everything again tomorrow just to make sure you haven't overlooked anything important.

• *Friday 24 November* •

Are you prepared to pull out all the stops today? Then you'll make a tremendous impression on someone, and that's very good news if you want to get this person on your side or win their admiration. It's also a very good day for sorting out a money matter, particularly if it has official overtones or requires very careful thought.

• *Saturday 25 November* •

Get set for a day of interruptions and distractions. It will be hard to settle down to anything for long, partly because the phone could keep ringing or someone may keep asking you questions, and partly because you're not really in the mood for concentrated bursts of work. Someone could have some strange suggestions now that mystify or puzzle you, yet there are reasons why you feel unable to ask them what they're talking about.

• *Sunday 26 November* •

Someone is very kind and considerate towards you today, and you'll feel very grateful to them especially if they belong to the realms of officialdom. If you've been burning the midnight oil recently, or working your socks off trying to meet a deadline, give yourself a breather at some point today even if you also have to do some work. Otherwise, you'll start to feel like a piece of chewed string.

• *Monday 27 November* •

The more inventive you are today the happier you'll be, so be prepared to depart from the straight and narrow every now and then. If you need to sort out a financial matter you could find that it helps to approach the whole thing from a new angle. It will also help to talk to an official as though they're a human being rather than someone sent to make your life a misery.

• *Tuesday 28 November* •

Money burns a big hole in your pocket today, especially if you've decided to beat the rush and start your Christmas shopping. You could get so carried away buying presents that you choose several for yourself! That's great if you can afford it but it's not such good news if you're trying to stick to a budget and not go over it. Alternatively, it's your partner who'll make free with the joint account.

• *Wednesday 29 November* •

You're in an adventurous mood today, so be prepared to live a little. Maybe you're dreaming about your next holiday and you can't keep away from those holiday brochures. Love could enter your life today in the guise of someone from another country or culture. You'll find them very attractive even if you can only admire them from afar. Oh well!

• *Thursday 30 November* •

End the month on a high note by getting together with some of your favourite people. Choose friends and loved ones who are always interesting to talk to or who've lived fascinating lives. You're certainly not in the mood for anyone who's only got one topic of conversation or who's a little bit slow on the uptake. If you meet someone new today you'll be intrigued by them.

DECEMBER AT A GLANCE

Love	♥ ♥ ♥ ♥
Money	£ $ £
Career	💻 💻 💻
Health	☼ ☼ ☼

• *Friday 1 December* •

Take it gently today because a certain someone isn't the easiest person to get along with. They could pour cold water over all your suggestions, or they may be very stand-offish and remote with you. Rather than make yourself miserable with them, you might prefer to spend time alone, concentrating on a project or venture that boosts your self-confidence and gives you something much more interesting to think about.

• *Saturday 2 December* •

What have you got lined up for today? If your heart sinks at the prospect of your usual Saturday routine, how about changing it in some way? Any departure from your normal schedule will lift your spirits and it might also fill you with excitement. Go on, be daring and do something different for a change! If you're at work you could come up with some wonderful ideas that leave everyone spellbound.

• *Sunday 3 December* •

Just in time for the festive season, the stars are urging you to think carefully about your finances throughout the rest of the month. It's especially important to concentrate on the money that you share with your other half, particularly if you have a joint account. Sort out any problems now, before they have the chance to get any worse. It's a great day for working on your Christmas budget so you know what you can afford to spend.

• *Monday 4 December* •

The air is full of emotional intensity today, making you take a close relationship very seriously. You could feel very worked up about an intimate alliance, especially if you're aware that there's room for improvement. So why not take advantage of today's mood to discuss what's wrong and find ways of making things better? If you meet someone new today, they'll have a profound impact on you.

• *Tuesday 5 December* •

Start thinking about what you want to achieve in 2001. Is there something that you've always wanted to learn or investigate? If so, now's your chance to find out more about it and, perhaps, determine to sign up for an evening class or workshop. A serious discussion with someone helps you to understand one another better now, and it might even be the key to a closer relationship in the future.

• *Wednesday 6 December* •

Have you started writing your Christmas cards yet? If you haven't even bought them, this is the day to get cracking because you're in exactly the right mood. A hunch or flash of inspiration will pay off wonderfully well, especially if you're working on a career plan or you're busy sorting out some official money matters. Take the time to listen to someone in authority – you'll start to understand what makes them tick.

• *Thursday 7 December* •

You're feeling very lucky today, so it's a great opportunity to put this to the test. It's an especially fortunate day for money matters and someone might do you a big financial favour. Be careful if you're expected to sign an agreement or fill in a complicated form because you may be overlooking some rather important information. Make a special effort to read the small print, even though it's boring!

• *Friday 8 December* •

You've got friends in high places this month, as you'll soon discover. It's a marvellous time to improve your relationships with people in power. That means you might chat to your boss or make an effort to get on better with a superior. Charm also opens many doors now, particularly if you want to get ahead in your career. Watch out for someone who could be a bit of a gold-digger or who's more interested in your power than your personality.

• *Saturday 9 December* •

It's the perfect day for making long-range plans, especially if they're connected with your finances or your goals and ambitions. You're full of high hopes and you're feeling quite inspired, so think carefully about what you want to achieve. You could also discover a belief or philosophy now that gives you tremendous emotional satisfaction or which answers some of the questions you've been asking yourself.

• *Sunday 10 December* •

Money burns a hole in your pocket today, so go carefully if you're feeling broke or you're trying to count the pennies. If you're feeling flush, however, you'll really enjoy buying something that boosts your self-confidence or improves your image. Maybe you fancy buying a new outfit, all ready for the approaching party season, or perhaps you'd prefer to have a blitz on the Christmas shopping?

• *Monday 11 December* •

Today's Full Moon is rather timely because it concentrates on your finances. In fact, it's telling you that this is the ideal time of the year to think carefully about your money matters and to tie up any loose ends that threaten to trip you up. Pay any outstanding bills now, in case you forget about them in the run-up to Christmas. It's also a great opportunity to make any New Year resolutions that have a financial slant.

• *Tuesday 12 December* •

Take care if you're involved in something connected with bureaucracy or big business today because it will be easy for someone to pull the wool over your eyes or give you only half the story. That's because you're in a very receptive and easy-going mood, and you're inclined to think the best of people instead of being wise to the games they may be playing. Someone in authority is very kind to you today.

• *Wednesday 13 December* •

You're in a very practical frame of mind, which is just what you want if you're hoping to get a lot done today. It's the ideal opportunity to get out your Christmas list and tick off a few more items. It's also a great day for writing an important letter or making a vital phone call. If you're attending a meeting or interview, you'll impress everyone with your quietly confident grasp of the situation.

• *Thursday 14 December* •

Have you got a stack of work waiting for you today? If so, the bad news is that you're not really in the mood for it. You may not even have a lot of energy, and you'd much rather take things easy and do something enjoyable. Try to get the chores over as soon as possible so you can spend plenty of time relaxing. A woman may be difficult to handle, especially if she seems jealous or competitive. What's she up to?

• *Friday 15 December* •

The more lively things are today, the better you'll like them. So try to ginger things up if they threaten to become rather tedious or predictable. A partner or boss is like a breath of fresh air now because they're full of good ideas or they show a new side to their personality. If you're looking for a new job, you could spot something that's a complete departure from your current career but which is very interesting.

• *Saturday 16 December* •

It's one of those days when you need to keep a firm hand on the financial tiller, otherwise you could get into deep water when you spend more than you intended. It's certainly a day when the shops are calling you, and if you've got the money to spare you'll have a ball. Catch up with your Christmas shopping or buy yourself a few treats.

• *Sunday 17 December* •

You can establish a great rapport with someone today, especially if you recently fell out with them or you don't always see eye-to-eye. Make an effort to understand them and see things from their point of view. It's also a great day for sorting out your social life for the rest of the month. Arrange to meet some of the people you haven't seen recently.

• *Monday 18 December* •

Have you got a long list of things that you want to get done before Christmas arrives? Then you'll be able to pull out all the stops today because you're feeling very industrious and methodical. If you're working as part of a team you'll really pull your weight, and you could also lend a hand if someone is struggling on their own. Make the most of your current surge of confidence as well.

• *Tuesday 19 December* •

It's another day when you're able to achieve a lot if you're at work. You could also make a tremendous impact on someone you meet now, whether you're getting together for business or pleasure. If you're involved in a financial negotiation at the moment you'll enjoy bargaining or haggling today. There could also be a frisson of intense emotion between you and a certain person that you meet through your work.

• *Wednesday 20 December* •

Someone really makes your day when they thank you for all your hard work or show their appreciation with a bonus, tip or present. It's an excellent day for attending a job interview or assessment, because you're a very impressive proposition at the moment. It's also a good day for having a serious talk about a medical matter or for booking that check-up with the doctor or dentist.

• *Thursday 21 December* •

Life begins to offer all sorts of wonderful opportunities from today, and it will stay that way for the next four weeks. You're filled with a spirit of adventure, making you want to spread your wings and take off in new directions. It's the perfect time to begin planning your New Year resolutions, especially if these involve learning more about the world. Be prepared to grab the opportunities that are just around the corner. Who knows where they could lead!

• *Friday 22 December* •

Is this your last day at work before the festivities? If so, you're feeling very businesslike and will want to tidy up all the loose ends before you begin your Christmas holiday. Make the most of your good ideas now because your brain is working well and you could come up with some red-hot suggestions. It's a very good day for having an in-depth discussion with someone about a subject that's dear to your heart.

• *Saturday 23 December* •

Partnerships start to come under the spotlight from today, and you'll want to channel a lot of energy into your one-to-one relationships during the next few weeks. You're very keen now to get on well with other people, but watch out for a slight tendency at times to come on too strong or to try to force the issue. You could feel impatient when people don't agree with you but try to give them some leeway.

• *Sunday 24 December* •

It's Christmas Eve and you're probably rushing around like mad, trying to get everything ready. However, be prepared for an older friend or relative to alter some arrangements at the last minute or drop a bombshell. If the family are all together, someone could act out of character or take pleasure in being a bit contrary. You might also have an unexpected visitor.

• *Monday 25 December* •

Happy Christmas! It promises to be a very significant day because there's an important New Moon today and it's offering you some wonderful opportunities during the next couple of weeks. You're in a very light-hearted and expansive mood, so you stand every chance of having a really good time. The more laughter there is today, the better you'll like it.

• *Tuesday 26 December* •

You're still in a great mood and you're all set to enjoy yourself. It's a lovely day for getting out of the house and doing something different for a change, especially if you could do with some fresh air. Go for a long walk with some friends or the family, or immerse yourself in a fascinating book. Make the most of your current feeling of optimism.

• Wednesday 27 December •

Even though you're still in the middle of the festivities, your mind is already straying to the future. It's a great day for arranging something that you can look forward to, especially if it involves a mental or physical journey. How about planning your next holiday or thinking about taking a weekend break? You're definitely in the mood to broaden your horizons now.

• Thursday 28 December •

Go carefully today because a certain person is very difficult to handle. They seem to have got out of bed the wrong side this morning, and now they're finding fault with people or biting everyone's heads off. Better keep out of their way! If you're fed up with a certain person's behaviour, you may be provoked into telling them what you think. At least you'll be able to clear the air.

• Friday 29 December •

What's up? You're feeling rather downcast or miserable today. Has reaction set in after all the festivities of the past few days or are you bothered about the way a certain person is treating you? It's tempting to imagine that things are worse than they really are now, and it's also very easy to feel that people are out to get you. But are they? Try to keep a sense of perspective. It may help to confide in someone.

• Saturday 30 December •

You're feeling dynamic and energetic, so thank goodness yesterday's morose mood has evaporated. It's a wonderful day for concentrating on your long-term hopes and wishes and deciding what you want to achieve in 2001. Start writing down your ideas or discuss them with someone who can help you to turn them into reality. You're also feeling very sociable, so try to get together with other people whenever you get the chance.

• *Sunday 31 December* •

It's a lovely end to the year because you're feeling outgoing and gregarious. Perfect, in fact, for attending a party or having a private celebration. If you're being sociable, you could meet someone very interesting and they might even become a new chum. If you enjoyed working on your New Year resolutions yesterday, carry on today because you'll come up with some inspired ideas.